Instructor's Guide for

# NEW WORLDS OF LITERATURE

## Jerome Beaty
*Emory University*

## J. Paul Hunter
*The University of Chicago*

W · W · NORTON & COMPANY
New York • London

Printed in the United States of America

W. W. Norton & Company, Inc.
500 Fifth Avenue, New York, NY   10110

W. W. Norton & Company, Ltd.
37 Great Russell Street, London WC1B 3NU


ISBN 0-393-95761-6


    3 4  5  6  7  8  9  0

Contents / iii

Contents / iv

# 1
## HOME

Familiarity may be a liability as well as an asset to your students in this section simply because the themes and subjects are so accessible that reading the selections here may not strike them as reading literature. The exotic settings in some selections may help. For non-Caribbean students, the unfamiliar vegetation and landscape (and the customs specific to the islands) in the first selection may give the jolt of unfamiliarity that will make the selection seem "important" enough to read in a college class. But there are also important teaching advantages in having the early readings seem both familiar and ordinary in their themes and interests. New Worlds of Literature has been designed to minimize the fears many students have of literature by "mixing" different kinds of selections-- stories, essays, poems, autobiographical narratives--so that students will feel that they are reading about something (in the case of this chapter, something so ordinary that the readings will not run much danger of seeming "privileged," "elitist," or even "literary") rather than reading less familiarly in a set form. We will make suggestions later about how to make--within the textbook's plan--literary distinctions of form and mode. You may, of course, depending on the emphases you want to create in your particular class, wish to make your students conscious of some formal distinctions (about the particular demands of verse, for example) early on, but for most freshman courses in writing or in reading we think that technical and formal distinctions had best come later.


## Michael Anthony
## SANDRA STREET

Short story; Trinidadian*
Setting is an obvious thing to emphasize in teaching this story, for there are plenty of physical details important to the narrative, and in a very real sense the story is about setting--the narrator's sense of place as he becomes self-conscious about differences between the section of town where he lives and other sections distinguished by different appearances, customs, and economic contexts. Several of the study questions (here,

---

* Ethnic characterizations in the guide refer to the author's background as reflected in the particular work and are intended only for quick reference.

as elsewhere in this text, placed just after the story) will raise a number of issues of setting for your students. Most of the questions, by the way, will almost answer themselves in the text itself. They are designed primarily to get your students into the habit of reading closely and precisely and then to think about larger issues. Beyond the facts of the story, the questions point primarily to questions that will help get the story's themes and effects into perspective. Assigning some or all of the questions before class is one possibility, of course. Another way of using the questions is as a basis for essays or other short writing assignments. We have tried to ask the kind of questions that you can easily adapt to writing assignments. At the end of each chapter are suggestions for a variety of kinds of papers--analytical, critical, argumentative, personal, parodic--that often involve comparing one selection with another. Most of these topics are also "adaptable" to other uses, and you will probably think of many ways to apply them to different selections and to issues particular to your own course and your specific emphases. We hope the questions will be suggestive to you and stimulate your own creativity, though we have also tried to offer a few cut-and-dried suggestions for those moments when you haven't time to develop a topic of your own.

If you do decide to discuss setting in "Sandra Street" in class, you might want to get into a discussion of temporal as well as spatial setting. And this can early lead to a discussion of perspective, point of view, and focus. We take up these matters later (in the afterword to chapter 4), but you might wish to look briefly ahead to that issue if your students are experienced enough at this point to handle it, or just to talk about (without using any technical language) the implied differences in years between the narrator as observer and the narrator as a later meditator on events of long ago. Questions 8 and 9 will set this up for discussion.

But begin with elementary issues about setting. Ask them which details of physical setting they remember best and why, and which details seem most important to the narrator. Ask which ones imply economic and social status, which tell us most about the narrator's values and feelings. Ask what details they do not see recorded that they might like to know about. Ask why so much detail is given about the teacher. Ask how they know how to read the details, that is, how they conclude what the meaning of a particular detail is, how they decide which ones are really important.

Ellen Gilchrist
TRAVELER

Short story; Regional
     One nice thing about teaching this story early is
that it gives students a chance to feel vastly superior
to a character without having to condescend to the story,
for what they really feel superior to here is an earlier
version of themselves.  Again, setting is a good issue
for discussion because the two settings in the story
provoke such different responses in the main character.
A good class discussion, involving issues of character as
well as setting, can be generated from questions about
what makes the Delta seem so exotic to LeLe.  Have them
compare the exoticism of setting in "Sandra Street," which
the narrator takes to be boring and shameful.  Setting
can move you quickly into a discussion of character here,
for the unfamiliarity that LeLe feels about her new
surroundings frees her from all sorts of accustomed
"limitations,"  even a consistent sense of herself.  <u>Who</u>
LeLe sees herself to be, and who she seems to us to be
can be readily gotten at by discussing how various people
in the story respond to her at various times. Get your
class to articulate exactly what characteristics and acts
of behavior produce particular responses in other
characters.


Luis Cabalquinto
HOMETOWN

Poem; Filipino-American
     This poem is easily accessible even to those who
have no experience in reading poetry, but its quiet
stasis may puzzle readers who expect story and movement
through time.  It is, in fact, a good poem to contrast
with narrative, for it suggests a different function that
poetry often performs--the isolation of a moment and an
elaboration of the feelings provoked by that moment.


Edward Hirsch
IN A POLISH HOME FOR THE AGED (CHICAGO, 1983)

Poem; Eastern-European-American
     Readers of traditional poetry will find a lot to
like here.  This poem virtually cries out for comparison
(and contrast) with morning poems in the aube and aubade
traditions, such as Richard Wilbur's "Love Calls Us to
the Things of This World" or Donne's "The Sun Rising."
But here the waking is to memories of long ago and far
away, to life tenaciously held instead of to a lover or
an intense youthful moment.  This is also a good

selection for beginning to confront the issues associated with cultural loyalties and the conflicts between values in different traditions.

The second word of the poem, "sweet," an odd word to use in the late 20th century, recalls the standard sense word used by Shakespeare and his contemporaries to collate all kinds of pleasant sights, sensations, and feelings. Here the memories that add up to sweetness are diverse, even odd, and one good way of getting at the character of the speaker is to let the discussion draw attention to the wild combination of memories and to get your students to put the consciousness together through the accumulation of moments remembered. Because most of the poem contrasts vivid communal memories of the past with stark and lonely conditions in the "home," students are apt, at first, to think of the poem as a piece of elderly nostalgia. Get them to detail the contrasts first, then lead them to talk about attitudes toward the present. Where is the expected bitterness, the put-down of modernity? Where does the vividness of memory come from? How is it related to the acceptance of a present which, for all its sense of loss, still retains vitality of mind? The key to teaching this aspect of the poem is, I think, to pick just the right moment in the discussion to ask them just what the last stanza of the poem means, how the old advice relates to the speaker's attitudes now toward the savoring of moments and getting pleasure out of a combination of past and present. Then go back to "sweet" and all the different things it stands for.

Cathy Song
HEAVEN

Poem; Chinese-American

Because poetry often seems difficult and alien to inexperienced readers, one way of discussing a poem like this one is to get your students, at first, to talk about the narrative elements. Here are three characters--the "dreamer" son, the speaker, and the grandfather pictured primarily as a boy--plus two vivid settings and a plot connected over three generations. But there is no story, only conclusions and feelings. What are the people like? How are the connections between them made with little or nothing "happening" in the poem? How are the interests here different from those in a story? How are the elements of character, setting, and plot handled differently?

Lee Ki Chuck
FROM KOREA TO HEAVEN COUNTRY

Interview; Korean-American
     Get your students to discuss fully how they <u>feel</u>
about Lee Ki Chuck.  You will probably find a wide range
of opinions of him.  My students find it hard to like
him, and I usually end up taking his part, with minimal
support from a few other defenders.  The key to teaching
this surprisingly complex narrative successfully is, I
think, to get students to tie their responses to the
language in the piece.  Ask just what attitudes bother
them (or which they admire).  What expressions embed
themselves in memory?  How do they feel about the way he
repeats himself?  Which representations are least
sympathetic?  Do they look down on his difficulties with
the language?  What values do they associate with the
ability to control language in self-presentation?
     Have them compare the meaning of "heaven" here with
that in Cathy Song's poem.  Get them to account for the
differences, and help them make categories for the ways
they do it, in terms of character, culture, belief,
tradition, literary mode, etc.


Agha Shahid Ali
POSTCARD FROM KASHMIR

Poem; Kashmiri-American
     This poem, like the one that follows, makes a good
study in memory.  The study questions here can guide the
discussion to issues of the meaning of the past for each
speaker.


Michael Blumenthal
WASHINGTON HEIGHTS, 1959

Poem; German Jewish-American
     The poems by Blumenthal and Song and the oral prose
selection by Lee Ki Chuck work well together as a unit
because the issue of language control is so prominent in
all three.  In each case, the issues of feelings about
home, while ultimately dependent on powers of observation
of physical detail, seem heavily dependent on the
speaker's ability to control language.  Blumenthal's poem
may seem to some students almost too controlled:  every
detail is thoroughly remembered and savored, every word
is calculated, everything adds up, all is ultimately
understood.  Of course, these qualities are, in part,
what makes it such a finished (and, I think, emotionally
powerful) poem, but the "art" is more prominently in view
here than in some selections.  Song's poem, equally

carefully crafted, may seem less controlled, and Lee Ki
Chuck's seems "natural."  Get your students to pin down
exactly how they determine the calculation and art.
Smoke out their values and make them self-conscious about
them.  These three selections, quite beyond their
literary value and their uses in suggesting different
attitudes toward place and culture, can be very helpful
to students in seeing themselves more closely and
understanding how the responsive process works for
readers.
     "Washington Heights, 1959" is a good poem to come
back to (or use right now) to explore issues of speaker,
especially to illustrate how a double consciousness
(then/now) can be used to offer perspectives on childhood
events.  Compare "Sandra Street"; contrast "Traveler."
Notice the very different uses of memory in Hirsch.  The
study questions provided here will set up your students
for this kind of discussion.


                    Vanessa Howard
          ESCAPE THE GHETTOS OF NEW YORK

Poem; Afro-American
     This poem "looks" more improvisational than earlier
poems in this chapter--Blumenthal's, for example--and you
can get good mileage in class out of its formal features.
Not only are its image patterns structured and its words
carefully chosen, but its vividness is carefully built
into a series of visual "takes."  The colloquialism, the
apparent informalities of speech become absorbed into a
careful (and very satisfying) structure that distances
the speaker from the chaos of its subject.  This is a
good poem to use to suggest the difference between the
subject matter a poet begins with and what can be done
with it.


                    Lance Henson
              poem near midway truck stop

                    Carter Revard
              DRIVING IN OKLAHOMA

Poem; Native American (Cheyenne)
Poem; Native American (Osage)
     Both these poems individually generate good class
discussion in a  pure "close analysis" exercise in
reading.  But they also work well taught together in a
comparative exercise.  Their superficially similar
subject matter--a momentary experience on roads in
Oklahoma--provides material for very different poetic
effects. Ask your students about the language in each

poem: why does Henson strip down vocabulary to the most
basic elements to get his effects while Revard builds a
rich fabric of metaphor and vivid visualization?   Use
the language to lead your students to talk about what
different effects the two poems strive for.


Neil Bissoondath
THERE ARE A LOT OF WAYS TO DIE

Story; Trinidadian-Canadian
     It's useful early in class discussion here to go
back to "Sandra Street." Not only are the settings
similar and both authors concerned with exploring
stereotypical attitudes toward insularity but
both stories also work carefully with contrasts (but
for very different effects) between younger and older
responses to island habits and values.   Another
productive way to discuss this story is to compare the
plot of the story itself with the plot Joseph dreams in
his early life and in his decision to return.   Still
another good classroom discussion can be generated by
looking carefully at how Pacheco House works as an object
to focus the narrator's sense of place.   (You may want to
return to the story again when you are discussing some of
the family encounters in later narratives and look
carefully at the scenes between Joseph and his wife.)


Elena Padilla
MIGRANTS: TRANSIENTS OR SETTLERS

Nonfiction; Puerto Rican-American
     "Evidence" is a good subject for discussion here.
Once your students have described the essayistic and
academic uses of evidence here to your satisfaction, you
might get them to compare how narrative writers
(Bissoondath or Gilchrist, for example) use evidence to
develop their themes.   The strategies in argumentative
(or "proof") modes, have more to do with rhetorical
signals ("for example," "in one case," "according to a
study of . . ." ), and evidence in stories tends to seem
to be only detail. Have them list the "evidence" about a
character or the character of a place in a story and look
for signals that it is being used to perform an
evidentiary function.

Louise Erdrich
INDIAN BOARDING SCHOOL: THE RUNAWAYS

Poem; Native American (Chippewa)
The study questions here will set up a discussion of
how language and detail lead to mood and effect. It may
be worth a fair amount of class time to clarify the
precise effect of different individual words--*stumbling,
lame, dumb, frail*--and the prevailing imagery of injury
and loss.


Maurice Kenny
GOING HOME

Poem; Native American (Mohawk)
A good selection to return to the theme of "home."
Several selections in the chapter involve either a real
or a metaphoric return to an earlier home. Contrast the
homecoming here, for example, with that in Bissoondath
(but notice how similarly this poem and that story image
the confines of home). Compare the metaphoric homecoming
in Song's "Heaven" or Blumenthal's "Washington Heights,
1959."


Lorna Dee Cervantes
FREEWAY 280

Poem; Chicana
Compare the "scar" imagery here to that in the
Erdrich poem above. Compare the function of the road
here to that in the poems by Erdrich, Revard, and Henson.
What different feelings does the road represent in the
different poems? Get your students to point to how the
language of each poem leads to a sense of what the road
represents.


Wakako Yamauchi
AND THE SOUL SHALL DANCE

Play; Japanese-American
Staging this play offers interesting problems of
interpretation. It is almost always a good idea to
generate a discussion, early on, of visual and theatrical
effects when you first begin discussing a play. Here the
thing to concentrate on, especially if you have been
tracing the "home" theme in this chapter, is the way the
two house settings are presented. I have had good luck
getting students to sketch out visually--on paper if they
are shy, on the blackboard if it is a bold, outgoing
class--the way they would want the set to look at key

points in the play.  Having students "cast" the play
often yields productive discussion, too; ask them what
impressions they want particular characters to create,
what body language they would have the actors use.


Audre Lorde
HOME

Poem; Caribbean (Carriacou)
    Compare the attitudes in this poem to those in
Bissoondath's story.  How, in each case, is the effect
produced?

# 2

# FAMILY DEVOTIONS

The first four selections in this chapter center on mothers, the next eight on fathers, and all are from the vantage point of the child or grown-up child. The next three are parental views of children, then the Maya Angelou selection about siblings (and their absent mother), and finally, the David Hwang play that gives this chapter its title and has children and in-laws, great-aunts and grandmothers, relatives of all kinds. Like the other selections in this book, they all involve, in varying degrees, American minority cultures or cross-cultural relations.

In a literature or writing course, then, the selections can be approached from either or both of these thematic angles. Though not mawkish or trite, the moving and loving Ardizzone story is closer to what we would conventionally expect in a story about one's mother, especially about a mother now dead. The Layton poem is more critical, almost hostile, and you may have to work at it a bit to show the love, pride, and admiration that shines through the tough, forthright description of her ferocity. Our students will see the love in Woo's "Letter" more readily, perhaps miss or forget the "generation gap" at the beginning; the talk about her own children adds a third generation to the family. Yvonne Sapia's poem should strike a chord in all our students (as well as in all of us): the mother is a particularized universal. The fathers are seen as heroic in poems by Schwartz and Liu, and seen tenderly in "The Gift": these tributes we should have no trouble with. The victimized stepfather in "Charlie-O" is treated with gentle love, but my experience is that students are very hard on losers, not yet having lost themselves, and hard on those they see as "weak." The unorthodox fathers, like the selfish Selbst in Bellow's story and the raffish father in the Baca poem may raise some hackles as well as eyebrows, and the latter raises as well the issue of whether parental neglect makes for strong children. The next three stories center on the child, from the newborn John to the grown-up "offspring."

### Tony Ardizzone
### MY MOTHER'S STORIES

Short story; Liechtensteiner- and Italian-American

Maybe I'm just getting older, but I remember the time when students used to complain that all English professors ever talked about was sex--and now it's death. Why is it, they ask, that all the things that are supposed to be good, and are in our books, are such downers--always about death and things like that?

So it is a bit of a risk to start off a course or even a chapter with a story that is, in effect, a prose elegy. But "My Mother's Stories" doesn't read or feel like a downer, even though it is framed at the beginning and end with the mother's death. Perhaps the story does not seem so dark because the first, throwaway scene is a triumph over death; the mother did not die as an infant, for she did, after all, become the narrator's mother. From the mother's first smile as she tells the story of her birth until near the midpoint of the story, her stories are about her life, dwelling on courtship and marriage, and, after the brief interruption in pars. 23-24--the birth of her first child--the narrator's childhood memories, and the mother's own memories of her childhood.

Your mother or the mother of some of your students may have died, and in the natural course of things mothers will die before their children, so the experience of the loss is universal if not entirely inevitable. Your students, the lucky ones who have not had to face loss so soon, will still, as young as they are, be aware that such a loss is likely to be in their future. Few students will find this story too far from their real or imagined experience.

The episode of the rabid dog ties together all the narrow escapes from death (par. 62), and the way dogs and the animal's face resonate with the mother's lupus drives us back at the end to the title--which, after all, is not just "My Mother"--and so to the recurrent passages about story-telling. This would be a good story to use to begin talking about stories. His mother's stories, the narrator says, have made her memory his memory (par. 4), so one of the functions of stories, it seems, is the transmission of experience or heritage. To tell a story well, you have to be more conscious of the story than of the audience--you have to imaginatively re-live it (par. 10). Yet stories are not merely recollections; the imagination must be brought into play and must, sometimes, rearrange the material--the story of the rabid dog, for example is "imagined": though it happened, it did not happen just the way the narrator tells it (pars. 57 and 65). But the use of the imagination and of restructuring reality is not for the purpose of withdrawal or evasion: the mother's stories are not veiled, nor is this one, though the narrator admits that other stories he has written have been veiled (par. 55). Directness is not an uncontrolled outpouring, however; some things, like the details of the mother's decline and death, are best withheld, just as the mother withholds details for effect.

Discussion of these details about the art of storytelling may help prepare students for writing a personal narrative. (The subject matter, too--mothers dead or alive; mother's stories, etc.--should be able to stimulate most students.)

Your students may not understand why the narrator's parents are thought of as having a "mixed" marriage. This is one of the several pieces in the volume--O. Henry's "The Coming-Out of Maggie" and Gabrielle Roy's "Wilhelm" in chapter 8, for example--in which the ethnic differences are in a rather narrow range and would scarcely be "mixed" in our more ethnically diverse culture. This might be a good occasion for the discussion of mini-mixed courtships and marriage--Irish and Italian, Sicilian and Liechtensteinian, where even the religion is shared, or Japanese-Chinese (Family Devotions), or Jewish-Christian ("A Silver Dish")--and to discuss current attitudes toward these matches compared to attitudes about Oriental and white ("Obachan," ch. 3), black and white (Wedding Band, ch. 8), or red and white ("Song of the Breed," ch. 7). You might ask your students whether they believe in "mixed" marriages and how they define them. You might generate more discussion (and combine the cultural and familial foci of this chapter) if you asked what would happen if they brought the Other home to dinner (and announced an intention to get engaged or married or begin a relationship).

The characterization I find most engaging and challenging in "My Mother's Stories" is that of the father. It might be worth a close look, detailed discussion, or a paper.

Irving Layton
KEINE LAZAROVITCH

Poem; Rumanian-Canadian

A eulogy it's not. Perhaps it will be difficult to convince students that it's all right not to speak entirely well of the dead, that it's all right, even, Whistler forgive us, to see unattractive qualities in one's mother. But most difficult of all, no doubt, will be to convince some that clear-eyed, more or less objective and critical evaluation can accompany deep and intense love. This contention should make for lively class discussion, especially if you zero in on mothers.

To get a discussion going here should be easy; getting back to the poem may be more difficult. You might want to point out that "lousiness"(1. 8) seems to set the tone for the whole poem--it seems to be almost a quote from the mother, down-to-earth and negative like much that the speaker says about his dead mother.  Use of such a word is unconventional in a poem like this, just as the tone of the poem is unconventional. The range of language in the poem is noteworthy--from the colloquial "lousiness" to the poetic image of Death the plagiarist (I make much of this image--plagiarism is not just a borrowing or stealing but also something of a desecration: Death has taken the thick, heavy black eyebrows that were beautiful and imposing while Keine Lazarovitch lived and put them prominently on her dead face where they seemed startling and not "dignified" at all) to the powerful image of her red blood, her vitality, draining away into the waters of the earth (just as, the unspoken analogy seems to suggest, ashes return to ashes and dust to dust).

Merle Woo
LETTER TO MA

Nonfiction; Chinese- and Korean-American

If you assign the Layton poem first, this essay/letter may be a little easier to get into: the first paragraph could well remind the student of the blame/praise of the poem. Here, however, the mother is alive, and so we can more readily allow the criticism. Indeed, the "failure of communication" or the "generation gap" dramatically rendered in paragraphs 2-4 could give you a good place to begin. Are there things in the conversations between Woo and her mother that remind the students of their conversations with their mothers? Do any of them have the same sense of exasperation? or a sense that the talk has not been talk at all but filling up time?

Do they think Layton or Woo harder on the mother? Woo's acknowledgment of the difficulties her parents had to face and of the advantages they gave her are more than somewhat undercut by the implied blame of her parents for her alcoholism: they passed on to her a feeling of self-contempt. What do your students think of that? You might want to point out that though low self-esteem is, indeed, often suggested as a cause of addiction or alcoholism, recovery begins and is reinforced, most authorities say, by the addict accepting responsibility for his or her own life. Do the students feel Woo is sloughing off responsibility? To what degree do they feel their parents are responsible for their children's flaws or shortcomings?

Woo's struggle against racism and sexism is presented in some detail and almost every sentence and surely every paragraph ought to give rise to some heated class discussion. If they found Woo's attitude toward her mother wrong, does that affect how they feel about Woo's causes? Are those who blame Woo more likely to be those who don't agreee wholeheartedly with her aims in the

first place? What image of Woo comes through in her
arguments for her cause? What do the feminists and
antiracist activists in your class think of the tenth
paragraph in which Woo says she'd work with anyone who
"shares her sensibility," meaning that she won't work
with sexist anti-racist men or racist anti-sexist women?
What are the limits of "purity" of purpose? of
networking?

You might want to ask your students to imagine Merle
Woo's household, perhaps to imagine Emily's and Paul's
conversation with their peers when mom isn't around,
perhaps even to have them write a "Letter to Ma."

To answer part of my own study question 5, I do
find the letter a bit patronizing, especially the last
sentence, but isn't it hard, when you know you're right,
not to be patronizing to someone you love but who does
not see the justice of your cause? I also find the letter
moving and challenging and worth reading, arguing with,
talking and writing about--and anthologizing.


Yvonne Sapia
DEFINING THE GRATEFUL GESTURE

Poem; Puerto Rican-American
Who cannot relate to the first verse paragraph? I
was told I had to clean my plate gratefully because I
wasn't a starving Armenian. I tell my kids that what
they're leaving on their plates could feed an East
African family for a week. Here, however, the children
are made to feel guilty not for their wasting food but
for their appetite, for eating food that they did not--as
their mother did when she was a child--earn by hard work.
And they are expected to express gratitude not only for
the food but for its preparation.

The mealtime ritual is so universal and the verse
form so loose, it is easy to let the discussion of the
subject matter absorb all the class's time and attention
and to ignore the subtle artistry of the piece.  Look at
the emphasis on "was she" at the end of the first verse
paragraph which sets up the comparison with this "us" in
the rest of the poem, or the pattern of religious
vocabulary and imagery--"reverent," "archetypal,"
"missionary's care"--culminating in the final verse-
paragraph: "ritual," "obedience," "supplicants,"
"guilty"--which turn the "solemn loaves of bread" and the
whole meal into a communion.

I like to let the thematic conversation, the
community of experience, take over for a good while and
only then say, "But this is a poem. Why is it a poem?"
Then I direct attention to language, imagery, word order,
and rhythm.

Rhoda Schwartz
OLD PHOTOGRAPHS

Poem; Russian-American

Our students--and some of you--do not remember
Humphrey Bogart or Marilyn Monroe alive, or even John
Lennon or Elvis. Watching them on the screen or
listening to their voices on records may not seem at all
spooky, and may seem more historical than nostalgic.
Somewhere I have a picture of my father when he was
twenty-two and slim and with a full head of wavy hair. It
looks like him--a little. Since I know I was young once
and am no more, I can almost believe he was young once--
almost. But it does seem like history.

Doesn't "Old Photographs" sound, for all its
admiration and tenderness, as if it is talking about a
historical figure rather than a father? Perhaps its sense
of remoteness is due to its treatment of events in Russia
as being as far away in space as in time. The poem seems
to me to have also the kaleidoscopic or montage effect of
history. It not only offers disjointed episodes but makes
photography (the sepia picture of the great-grandmother)
into a talking picture, then, apparently into a movie
(are the friends throwing rolls of film? is the father
laughing in another photograph?), and finally merges it
with a story her father told her.

Though there is wonderful narrative here, my
students do not want to talk only about the subject
matter, ignoring the artistry--the structuring of the
material into a poem--as they often do after reading the
Sapia poem. I have had reasonably good luck in having
them first try to identify what is description of a
photograph, what is memory, what is recollection of a
story told her by others, and so on.

As the third study question suggests, this piece
is rich in characterization. The image of the daring,
devilish, vital, idealistic, sensual Russian youth whom
the speaker knew as her father, a salesman in America of
imported goods, comes across graphically--almost
photographically--and I like to take some time in getting
the students to discover how that is achieved.

Cynthia Kadohata
CHARLIE-O

Short story; Japanese-American

This is, I believe, a good story in which to
concentrate on characterization, if such a discussion is
part of your agenda for the course you are teaching. As I
said before, I find my students rather quick to condemn
"weakness"; many of them, if they are not yet "winners,"
are sure they are not going to be "losers." The story of

a very short man who marries a woman he knows is already
pregnant by someone else, raises--and loves--her
daughter, puts up with his wife's infidelity (though he
does move the family away to try to separate her from her
lover), and loses her nonetheless in the end: for some of
us such a story will seem a pathetic tale. We will feel
deep sympathy for poor Charlie-O (O as in zero?), and the
final sentence--"Promise me you'll never break anyone's
heart"--is heartbreaking in its own right. The story
seems to be an initiation story in which the
stepdaughter-narrator learns the importance of being
gentle and true in relationships.

    If the class starts out that way, however, you might
want to make a case for the prosecution. He knew what he
was getting into and tacitly made a bargain. He married
above himself--he could not have won his wife if she had
had free choice; she paid the price, lived with him for
years and bore him children, and yet cannot be blamed for
escaping or attempting to escape a marriage that on her
part was loveless. Must we break our own hearts in order
not to break others'? "Love thy neighbor as--not better
than--thyself."

    If the class starts out the other way, you could
argue the sympathetic side: What evidence is there that
his wife never loved him? Is running out of gas or
getting lost a sure sign of ineptitude or unworthiness?
Haven't you ever run out of gas?

    This "cuckoo" theme appears very subtly in
"Sánchez," Richard Dokey's story that appears in chapter
9, again the focus being on the child. The two stories
could profitably be taught together.

    You might want to raise the question of whether
there is a submerged cross-cultural aspect to this story.
If not, why is virtually nothing made of that theme? Do
you assume the mother is also a Japanese-American? the
lover? that this is a thoroughly integrated, color-blind
society (or two societies--California and Arkansas)? I
don't pretend to know the answers to these questions--
they're those rare things in guides or manuals, real
questions. They might be worth thinking and talking
about, especially given the number of cross-cultural
works in this anthology and given the ethnic variety of
modern American society where racism remains a very live
issue.

Simon J. Ortiz
MY FATHER'S SONG

Poem; Native American (Navajo)
    The father's song of the final four verse-paragraphs
seems to merge with the speaker's voice of the first
verse-paragraph, a fusing emphasized by the opening and

closing lines: "Wanting to say things, / I miss my father tonight"; "and my father saying things." If you can get your class to argue about who says what, you can interject at some point another question: if there is ambiguity does that make this then a poor poem? And another: what is the effect of not knowing, or even hesitating before you decide whether the speaker or his father is speaking? And at least one more: suppose that ambiguity and that effect are intentional, what would that mean?

What would they say if you suggested that the fusing--or confusing--of the father's and son's voices, their "harmony," may, indeed, be the point and the achievement of this poem/song?


## Li-Young Lee
## THE GIFT

Poem; Indonesian-Chinese-American
     As "My Father's Song" does--the two poems bear comparison--this poem pays tribute to a father's strength, tenderness, and life-enhancing nature.

You might want to raise the question of whether the poem is sentimental or just deeply and appropriately moving. This might be a good piece--it's short enough to keep in mind in its entirety--to use to bring up the emotional impact of literature, and issues such as earned and unearned emotion. You are not likely to believe that you have a ready answer or infallible litmus test for sincerity or effectiveness, but we as teachers may as well show our feet of clay early on. There are better answers and worse answers, we know, but perhaps not definitively wrong answers and certainly not positively right answers to almost any worthwhile question. (That'll unsettle them, won't it; or will it unsettle your authority in the class more. It's a tough call.) Several times over the years when I've tried to handle the question of which evocations of emotion are appropriate and which are excessive and sentimental, I've been embarrassed to find that I was a sentimentalist, and at other times, I was cold and unfeeling. Nonetheless, it's a question we all need to take on once in a while, for the issue is a real one and as most real questions, significant, imperative, and unanswerable, but worth the discussion.

This poem seems relatively traditional in language and rhythm in the context of mid- to late-twentieth century American poetry, but to my ear or eye, the use and nature of the epithets in lines 28-30--"_Metal that will bury me_," "Little assassin," and "Ore Going Deep for My Heart" all seem somehow "foreign" or "Chinese." Do you feel this? Does your class? This seems to me one of the most exciting aspects of our cross-cultural literature, the two--or more--"voices" that speak through the lines of many "dual citizen-writers" of our society. Can't we often identify by intonation or certain tricks of syntax or vocabulary the ethnic roots of someone who was born in America and has no "foreign accent"? This other tune that blends with the "American" one is a kind of *dialogism*, a dialogic voice that promises a rich literary and cultural future.


Li-Young Lee
EATING TOGETHER

Poem; Indonesian-Chinese-American
    I hope your class doesn't meet right before lunch.
    I like to ask my classes whether they find the juxtaposition of dinner and death "gross" or inappropriate. A surprising number do not (perhaps because they watch TV news while eating). It takes a little longer to get them to talk about how "life must go on" and the importance of family ritual. The mother is now head of the family and gets the sweetest meat (more of my students find eating the meat from the head of a fish "gross" than they do the mingling of meals and death); she has, in effect, taken the father's "place." Sometimes this newly structured family comes up for discussion and there is conjecture about how the survivors feel. I let it go on, for, though it's not in the poem it does seem to me part of the poem; that is, the understatement of the poem leaves the emotional responses out but almost underlines them as something left out, a gap meant to be filled by imaginative and affective readers.
        The father in death being like a snow-covered road puzzles lots of my students, so I make them look more closely at the last four words of the poem. Is he in death any more independent of his family? any less? Is his family more or less independent without him at the dinner table?
    If you taught the previous Lee poem and talked about sentimentality, you could ask here whether his survival-of-the-living, independence-of-the-dead isn't the opposite, a little too hard-nosed. (In case you're interested, I don't think so, but I said above there are not any infallible tests for such judgments [just good taste, Buster].)
        (I haven't written Li-Young Lee, so I don't know if "him" in l. 11 is a misprint, a mistake, or a deliberate bit of poetic license used for the sound or to attract attention. )

Saul Bellow
A SILVER DISH

Short story; Jewish-American
"A Silver Dish" is not everybody's cup of tea.
Many students find it very difficult. It's not that
it's particularly esoteric or allusive--it requires only
two informational footnotes--and the frame of reference
does not seem particularly "arty." It is, however,
sophisticated and worldly. From the very first paragraph,
what with Lufthansa pilots in Aden and peristalsis, the
reader is expected to know something about the world he
lives in, if not necessarily about its high culture.
The real difficulty lies in its unconventional structure
and, even more, in its unconventional "morality" or world
view.
The structure, with its flashbacks and its shifting
from Woody's story to his father's, can be confusing. If
you've taught "My Father's Song," you might liken the
story's near-merger of father and son to that of the
poem, and explore what that identification and confusion
might reveal about the son's feelings for his father. (If
you put it that way, the students are liable to assume
you mean that since the son confuses himself with his
father it means unqualified love--they may not know about
Oedipus and the anxiety of influence.)
If I sense some confusion or impatient dismissal of
the story because of its "difficulty," I might ask the
class very early to unravel the events, writing out or
outlining the story not in terms of its structure
(par. 1-the end) but in terms of its <u>fabula</u> or history,
the chronology of the events as they are supposed to have
occurred. (Sometimes I suggest that they begin with par.
17--Morris Selbst's Polish-Jewish family abandoning him
in England.) I then like to have the students discuss <u>why</u>
the story seems structured as it is--hoping they will
bring up the sounding of the keynote of death in the
opening paragraph and the delayed introduction of the
incident of the silver dish, which, though it is narrated
very late in the story, happened years before, and
prepares the reader for the "trickery" of the final scene
in the hospital. (If they don't do so, I have to drag it
out or lay it out.)
Par. 17 is a good one to begin with in any case, for
it also introduces the unconventional morality--or
amorality--of Morris, perhaps that of Woody and maybe
even that of the story as well. ("At sixteen, scabbing
during a seamen's strike, he shoveled his way across the
Atlantic and jumped ship in Brooklyn. He became an
American, and America never knew it. He voted without
papers, he drove without a license, he paid no taxes, he
cut every corner.") You may have to insist the students
finish the paragraph too--he does love someone, two

people: Halina (who, of course, is not his wife) and Woody.

You may get a discussion going about the implied conflict in the story between morality and vitality. The story seems to suggest that the socially conventional peopl like Woody's mother (we also see her in par. 17) and the religiously conventional like his sisters are ignorant of what life is really like and live a sterile life in a dream world. Surely this won't go unchallenged (or undefended?). Those who are offended may well use this as a reason for not liking the story, which you might use, in turn, to bring up the whole issue of "belief" in the reading of literature. Do you have to be a Catholic to appreciate Dante, a Protestant to admire Milton, a Fascist or anti-Semite to like Pound? And how about the proposition that works that challenge your beliefs, if only to reinforce them, are more profitable than those that tell you that the way you look at things is the way any decent human being looks at things? (I have to watch out for discussions like this, however; I easily get led off the track.)

I like to have my students look back at Layton's poem earlier in this chapter (or I sometimes hold off assigning the Layton poem until just before this one) to compare the love and admiration of the parent's vitality amid the rather severe criticism of other aspects of their behavior in the two works. I also bring in "Charlie-O," which I suggest may be obliquely supporting the mother's sensuality and infidelity in the name of vitality, while sympathizing with the victim of that combination of traits, raising the whole issue of love versus morality.

This story ought to confuse and/or upset your students (and perhaps you?) enough to test your mettle as a teacher. I try to assign it when I feel the class is going well and when I feel I am in a good frame of mind for a profitable confrontation.


Jimmy Santiago Baca
ANCESTOR

Poem; Chicano
We meet here a rascally but vital and loved and admired father, like Woody Selbst's in "A Silver Dish." Thi poem can join that story and "Keine Lazarovitch" and "Charlie-O" in a discussion of morality and vitality, moral values and love.

I wonder whether one of this "gypsy-father's" daughters would write so admiring, loving a poem or whether they would think him a chauvinistic exploiter. Do your students believe the sons and daughters have "true freedom" (line 37) or truly understand love (l. 36)? How do they think this poem defines those terms? I have had some success in asking students to write a poem or brief prose piece about this "ancestor" from the silent grandmother's point of view (see lines 65-70).

Much of this poem seems to be written in a loose blank verse, but the lines about love and freedom are much longer. Does this seem to you to be significant? evidence that the poem is "protesting [or "attesting"] too much"? I've never tried talking about this in class; taught as part of the second chapter such a question may come too early in a course if this is the basic text and its order is being followed, but in the right class at the right time, it may be worth asking.

Stephen Shu Ning Liu
MY FATHER'S MARTIAL ART

Poem; Chinese-American
I like to teach this poem along with Lee's "The Gift," "Charlie-O," and, on a good day, "Letter to Ma," to explore (and to some degree explode) the stereotype of the Oriental macho, chauvinist male stereotype. Taught alone, this poem may tend to reinforce non-Asian views of what Asian gender values are. In context, not only do other works qualify that view but certain things show up--or seem to show up--in this poem that reading it as stereotypical may gloss over: saying he looks like a monk and stinks of green fungus is not exactly praise, even if the source is "only" a woman. The father's description of his Master's accomplishments goes beyond even the flashbacks in the old TV series "Kung Fu" in its apparent exaggeration--just maybe the chair trick (shades of "Karate Kid") and maybe splitting the cedar trunk (how thick a trunk?), but skipping over treetops like a squirrel? The son's description of the father's prowess seems a bit more credible.

And admirable. I don't mean to suggest the father is not loved and admired and praised. The expressed desire that he transcend these achievements, escape from death and hush the traffic is, of course, poignant. I try to get my classes to feel the emotions here as well as to analyze the possible exaggerations and qualifications.

I also like to ask them to look carefully at the topography in lines 22-23--how can you be on a busy street and "brood over high cliffs"?--and at the smog/smoke image of 11. 24-25. How do these images that contradict or transcend the physical and realistic make you feel? What do you infer from them about the son's/speaker's feelings? I ask.

Sherley Williams
SAY HELLO TO JOHN

Poem; Afro-American
    Is this a comic poem?
    See what happens if you start off with that
question. If things run true to form (and they usually
don't) the affirmatives will first cite the language
("I'mo"="I am going to"; "mo'n"="more than"; "pee" and
"ass"). Some negatives might object that this is racist,
that the affirmatives are making fun of Black English, as
if it were somehow inferior. With any luck, the defense
will cite the almost Anglo-Saxon strength (your term,
probably, not theirs, but you can help bring this out) of
one-syllable words like "bout," "tween," "cept," without
even the apology of an apostrophe. And though the lines
are loose--nothing unusual in contemporary poetry--the
xaxa rhyme scheme is traditional and disciplined,
including the strategically placed slant rhyme in the
middle stanza. Then finally, a joke, a smile, and a happy
ending, and you can get into comedy as both humor and
form or outcome.


Simon J. Ortiz
SPEAKING

Poem; Native American (Navajo)
    The suggestion in the editorial sentence at the top
of the poem might be a good way to open up the discussion
and to talk about expectation in lyric poetry as well as
in the narrative or dramatic forms. The first study
question can be used to open up the whole subject of
poetic form in free verse, for sometimes my students want
to know how something can be a poem if there isn't any
rhyme or regularity of meter.
    But I hate to use this lovely poem only to make
points about poetic form. Maybe it's the ham in me, but
this is one I really like to read aloud. It almost speaks
for itself, speaking of "Speaking."


Naomi Long Madgett
OFFSPRING

Poem; Afro-American
    This is the piece I use to open--or reopen--the
issue of the proper or healthy relationship of child and
parent. Students like it because the parental twig
bending does not make the child-tree grow the way
intended: the offspring does not, as the speaker
apparently intended, live her life to fulfill her

mother's self, but is successful, free, happy, in her own right and as her own self. How does the mother feel about her grown daughter? (Why must the speaker be the mother--because not many fathers are named Naomi?--but, then, we always have to remember that the speaker is not necessarily the poet.)

I hark back to "Letter to Ma" and try to bring up not only the obvious letter-writer-to-parent dimension, but the fact that Woo seems proud that her twigs have grown as bent. How much bending is good? Is keeping hands entirely off good parenting (remember "Ancestor")?

The unmetered, unrhymed form here is worth asking about too. I spend some time on timing or placement of words, for example, "self" (l. 8) and "unfamiliar" (l. 12) seem to apply as much to the daughter as to the street. Also worth examining are the final words of the last four lines and especially the final two one-word lines.


Maya Angelou
MY BROTHER BAILEY AND KAY FRANCIS

Narrative; Afro-American
I never know just how to start a class talking about this story so I often just give them their head or begin with that pedagogical banality, "How did you like this story?" (Actually, it's an excerpt from an autobiography, but if you're being banal, you might as well be sloppy as well.)

It is testimony to the power of Angelou's writing that more often than not the discussion takes off anyway, sometimes about the language. Most of my students love the richness of it, though sometimes the overtrained ask whether or not the first paragraph, comparing weekdays to "wheels," "rough drafts," and emerging from a "mold" is that violation of decorum known as a mixed metaphor. If that's the way they go, I ask them to hunt down all the figures they can and judge how well each one works and whether any seem to fail or to be reaching too much. Then I ask whether anything in the writing other than metaphor strikes them. Someone will usually point out the sentence in par. 10 that study question 1 points to, "Southern Blacks until the present generation could be counted among America's arch conservatives," and I ask them to look for more sentences like that until they come up with (or I point to), "Children's talent to endure stems from their ignorance of alternatives" (par. 5). These pithy aphorisms lead me to have them explore the focus and voice, the older narrator's stance and the younger girl's vision. I sometimes ask them to find five or six sentences that are clearly the words of the older

narrator and a few phrases other than dialogue that are
the narrator-as-a-young-girl.

If the initial dumb question is responded to with
the usual vague grunt of approval, "I like this story
because it's interesting," I pounce on that and ask why.
I am hoping to bring out the suspense when Bailey is
missing, the "mystery" when he offers no apologies, or
the poignant humor of the central episode of their
attraction to Kay Francis. If the occasion is right, I
try to get into the way we question narratives as we
read--What's going to happen next? What's happened
that causes this? and so on. I try not to let "It's
interesting" get away without having some discussion of
how the characters' feelings (especially Momma's early
and Bailey's in the second half of the piece) are
conveyed with little direct comment about or description
of feelings. (I can get into my "objective correlatives"
bit if I try hard enough.)

Sometimes the initial response centers on the
setting or context, on racism and the South "back then"
and on the items pointed out in study question 3. How
that takes off depends on the ethnic makeup of the
class--and on us.

David Henry Hwang
FAMILY DEVOTIONS

Play; Chinese- and Japanese-American
I like to assign plays one act at a time and to urge
students not to read past the act assigned. I can then
ask questions about what they anticipate will happen
next, how the play will develop and end with everyone
being equally in the dark (except us, of course, but I
try to stay out of the discussion of expectations but for
"why" and "what are you basing your anticipations on"
questions). When there is a conventional three-act
structure in modern plays (or five acts in Renaissance
plays), I ask about exposition, rising, and falling action
and so on. This, however, is a two-act play, and, despite
the fact that the two acts immediately follow each other
in time and take place on a single set, the two halves
are drastically different. There is all the more reason
then, it seems to me, to assign the acts separately and
to discuss Act I in terms of expectations before the
students have read Act II. In the following class period,
after they have read the second act we discuss how
surprised they were, how different the two acts are, the
effect of that difference; that is, to what degree it
"works," and so on. For the third class period--if I have
three to devote to the play, and I usually do--I ask them
to read the play again, this time picking out in the
first act all the indications of the kind of change that

happens in the second act (not necesarily foreshadowings of events, but of shifts of tone and the "register" of reality). I urge them, however, to read the second act as well and, knowing the shift will come and having noted that the tone of the first act is ambiguous or foreshadows the shift, to decide whether the shocking shift now seems more acceptable, less outrageous--and more meaningful (meaning in both the thematic and affective sense).

If it seems suitable with the particular class and the point we have reached in the course and the kinds of discussions we have had to date, I use the experience of this play to explore what happens when we reread things or to ask about the post-reading or post-viewing experience. The next day, are their feelings about and understanding of a work the same as they were the minute the movie or play was over, the minute they finished reading the story or novel? What happens after the reading? I try to get them to talk about re-running the reading experience like re-running a film: do they review or re-imagine the play from beginning to end? from end back to the beginning, like a rewinding? Do they pick out certain passages or scenes to think about? Do they pick the passages or scenes to "reread" or "resee" in the order in which they appeared or do they juxtapose scenes, episodes, lines from different parts of the work? If they, or at least some of them, say they pick and choose bits to remember, but not necessarily in the order in which they appeared, I pounce: This is what is meant by spatial order, I say, some sort of distortion or restructuring of the temporal or sequential order of the work and our reading or viewing experience of it. If conditions are right, I go on to talk about how authors structure or restructure works--by selections, rearrangement, and so on--and the similarity of restructuring to what we do in our memory of a work. It's really a different work, I suggest, there's really no such thing as a second reading or second viewing, if "second" means more or less identical repetitions of the experience and understanding of the work.

But all the preceding paragraph is governed by its first word, "If." More usually I ask various members of the class to read aloud from the first scene before the play has been assigned. And then again--not necessarily the same readers, but not necessarily different ones either--in the next class, after the first act has been read, we read the first part of the first scene again. I then ask the class to describe and discuss the differences between the two readings and to try to account for the differences. And I repeat the performance the next class period, after everyone has read the entire play.

Then, in this context, I bring up such things as those in the first study question--the relevance of the use of both Chinese music or chanting and of rock 'n' roll. The contrast means a lot more when it is seen in relation to the shocking shift in tone between the acts (or, to put it another way, the significance or foreshadowing of the music is lots clearer). It also allows me to ask about the relevance or suggestiveness or foreshadowing of the seemingly comic opening episode with the burnt chickens (sacrifices?) and the possibility that the dead chicken is Chickie. In the light of later events, the Chinese-Japanese banter may seem more ominous ("laugh and kill" may even describe the play!).

# HERITAGE

### Countee Cullen
### HERITAGE

**Poem; Afro-American**

The problem with this poem is <u>tone</u>. Perhaps I should say <u>my</u> problem with this poem is understanding its tone. I really do not know how Cullen answers the question "What is Africa to me?" (as you can probably detect in the study questions). So it is not difficult for me to begin the class with that question and to sit back and listen. I try to find students with alternative readings--it usually isn't hard:

> (1) the poem says "I am an African. My American, Christian self is merely a veneer. My real self is vital, responding to the rhythms, the drums of Africa" (ll. 80-82, 89, 96-98, e.g.). He surely does not want to quench his pride or cool his blood (l. 119); do we?

> (2) the poem says, "I am a Christian and have rejected the African gods (ll. 89-92), and therefore Africa; and though Africa is, of course, in my blood and dreams, it is not in my self and soul. It would be easier if Christ were black, and He and therefore I could be rebellious, but I am nonetheless Christian and must maintain my patience and peace" (ll. 101-16).

Both sides might want to use the last three lines, side 1 arguing that they are ironic, almost sarcastic, and side 2 arguing that they are straightforward. Since I am not a partisan of either side, I feel my role is just to remind the class that this poem was written more than sixty years ago and that they might ask whether they are not reading into the poem some of the values of the past twenty years or so--the celebration of the primitive or "earthy" racial pride, the downplaying of "civilized" ("bourgeois") behaviors and values.

With this lead, I can introduce the issue of historicism or "receptionalism." Should we try to understand a work as contemporaries understood it (or as we understand contemporaries understood it) or must it, if it is to last and be universal, <u>mean</u> something for us?"

Then, my pride makes me think that the reason I cannot decide just what side the poem comes down on is that it really concerns being caught between two worlds. The poem's strength comes from the powerful pull of the two forces, neither of which can dominate. The final

lines, then, are both straightforward and ironic--
whatever name that tonal ambivalence may have.

(I sometimes introduce here, as I do inevitably
somewhere, Gombrich's [or Wittgenstein's] use of the
rabbit-duck, that figure which can look like a duck's
head and bill or a rabbit's head and ears. But it can
only look that way alternatively, not simultaneously.
Perhaps this poem can be either an African rabbit or a
Christian duck, but not both at the same time.)


### Lorna Dee Cervantes
### HERITAGE

Poem; Chicana
     This brief poem raises many complex issues or
questions. The Chicana poet says she is treated
contemptuously by Mexicans when she returns to her
ancestral home. Blacks often are shocked by their
rejection by Africans (often being considered "white"--
i.e., not African). Some Asian cultures--the Indian and
Japanese, for example--also look down in various
ways on their American progeny, or so many report. Yet
Americans of European heritage seem to be readily
accepted by their family's native land (though some
report that the Irish think American Irish too "Irish").
Have you or members of your class heard such stories? How
do you account for it? Is it exported racism or
prejudice--i.e., those who are discriminated against here
are looked down upon by the country of their family's
origin?
     Do any of your students resent the tone of this
poem? Do they feel that the speaker should not expect to
have it both ways--either she(?) is Mexican or American?
     This could be a good piece, short as it is, to talk
about the sometimes painful feeling of the American
immigrants of first, second, or third generation caught
between cultures--not fully accepted here yet unable to
go home again. You can also explore the possible
responses, from anger at America, their emigrating
ancestors, or their ethnic homeland, to regret,
nostalgia, or pride in their new citizenship.


### Linda Hogan
### HERITAGE

Poem; Native American (Chickasaw and mixed)
     When I can get to them in time, I like to stop my
students' reading before line 45. One way is to have the
poem read in class rather than assigned, ask the students
to cover the poem and only uncover one line at a time as
they read, and cry halt at l. 44. Then I tell them there

are only two more lines, lines that in some way summarize the poem or its attitude toward the mixed heritage of the speaker, and I ask them to <u>write</u> those final two lines. I have not had anyone even come close to Hogan's closure yet. This is my rather elaborate way of emphasizing the surprise in the conclusion and the complex, elusive tone of the poem. Another method would be to have one student read aloud each of the first four verse-paragraphs and discuss whatever differences in tone the reading revealed amd as another student to suggest alternative tones or ways of reading.

If the poem is simply assigned, one way to begin discussion might be to have students list all that the speaker says she got from her white mother and all that she got from her Native American father. Because of the progression or sequence in the poem, I assume that the grandmother in lines 21ff. is her father's mother—despite the blue eyes—so that the ethnic mixture is not quite half and half, but I am far from certain about this and it might be a point to discuss.

Obviously, more space is spent on the speaker's Native American heritage.  L. 30 suggests that, at least while with her Native American family, she was ashamed of her whiteness, but the details of her Native American heritage do not seem entirely laudable (or am I reading white values into the poem?). How do your students read the spilling of the black saliva onto the speaker's white shirt by her snuff-chewing grandmother? Was it an actual incident, do they think? Or is it a symbol of the grandmother "tinting" the speaker's "white" mind with Indian lore? Or both? Tobacco, the grandmother says, is great medicine (in both the phsycial and spiritual sense). So why is "That tobacco" (the cure? the snuff?) a "dark night" covering her?

I'm not sure I can answer these questions in ways that satisfy me, so I'll turn them over to you; now you can turn them over to your students.

Let me know how it all comes out . . . .

The three "Heritage" poems, if for no other reason than their common title, ask for comparison. Unintentionally on the part of the editors, they seem to have in common a resentment either of their heritage or of their new citizenship, returning us once again to the sometimes agonizing but often fruitful issue of ethnic or national loyalties. (President Truman once said Zionists cannot be loyal Americans, and some said that so-called "isolationists" who opposed President Roosevelt's tilting toward the Allies before we entered World War II were reluctant to oppose Germany either because they were of German heritage or, if they were of Irish heritage, because they did not want to be allied with Britain.)

Agha Shahid Ali
SNOWMEN

Poem; Kashmiri-American
    Only four of the twenty-four lines of the poem
concern the ancestor's relations to "women," but
frequently women students argue that this poem expresses
the intention of the modern speaker to change in his own
life the traditional, patriarchal treatment of women.
(They rebuff the argument that the lines they find most
important constitute only one-sixth of the poem by
pointing out that they are spatially as well as
thematically central.) Read thus, the last lines mean
that the speaker will change traditional ways even if it
means betraying his ethnic heritage ("last snowman,"
"melting shoulders").
    An alternative reading that comes up is both more
general and somewhat more respectful of the speaker's
ancestral heritage. He will live in the modern world or
grow ("ride into spring") with whatever he can retain of
his heritage ("their melting shoulders"), even though,
given the modern world (new world?) he may be the last
representaitve of his cultural tradition. The "central"
lines, these readers say, despite the imagery of freezing
women, are not pejorative. They argue that the ancestor's
wife lived into old age, "thawed" (survived, even
flourished), and cite the "good vibes" from the word
"clear."
    Sometimes I wait for the one reading and counter
with the other, but often both can be drawn out without
too much comment or commitment on my part.
    Regardless of their "loyalties," most students find
this poem powerful and strangely moving, strange like the
mysterious ancestor from Samarkand.


Wendy Rose
TO SOME FEW HOPI ANCESTORS

Poem; Native American (Hopi)
    This poem, like "Snowmen," speaks of the persistence
of the ethnic and cultural traditions of those long gone
in the young people of today. Here I like to ask students
to list--sometimes on paper--the ways in which the
tradition has weakened and the ways in which it persists.
As in the previous poem, the enduring influence or effect
of their ancestors is somewhat ambiguous and certainly
not entirely happy (as the indented question here seems
to suggest).
    Rock and stone are of course hard, persistent, and
the bedrock, as it were, of the world, but in addressing
the last study question you might check to see how many
students know or tried to find out who the Hopi are,

where their ancestral home is/was, and what that might
have to do with the imagery of the poem.


### Cathy Song
### LOST SISTER

Poem; Chinese-American

The Chinese jade in this poem, you might want to
point out, echoes the rock and stone of the Hopi poem
that precedes it. Moreover, the woman named Jade, after
the stone that makes men move mountains to attain it,
follows her Hopi sister who has been "chiseled / on the
face" of the ancestral world. But the Hopi daughters left
home as almost none of the Chinese ones did. You should
have no trouble eliciting indignant comments about the
traditional Chinese treatment of women. I like to hold
off the "achievement" lines, 21-25, at first. Then I ask
the students to contrast the hobbled Chinese women and
the free-striding Chinese-American women, stopping for a
time at line 36. I sometimes then skip to the final verse
paragraph and ask about the need for a jade link. At
first the answers usually center on nostalgia, roots,
heritage. That's when I start moving in the other
direction, first back to ll. 21-25: "Was there nothing
valuable in their lives in China?" Then I go on to the
third verse-paragraph--the imperfections of the Chinese
experience in America. Finally, I invite discussion of
the final five lines and of the tone of the poem as a
whole (sometimes asking for comparisons of the ambiguity
of almost all the heritage pieces).


### Alice Walker
### EVERYDAY USE

Short story; Afro-American

Up until now, all the "Heritage" stories have been
from the point of view of the person--usually the young
person--who has departed geographically, and usually
spiritually as well, from the "old ways." Here the focus
is on the older generation who stayed at home, and the
story is set at the old homestead. I have not yet taught
this story, and I am anxious to see if my young students
can be led, chiefly by the first-person narration, to
side with the country mother and not with the
sophisticated daughter.

I am hoping there will be a Wangero Leewanika
Kemanjo in the class; otherwise, I'll have to invent one.
Is this an Uncle Tom story, mocking black pride and
militancy, the rejection of white traditions and the
search for heritage in the African past? Isn't that a
more honorable history than that of the 300-odd years in

America, years of slavery, discrimination, deprivation and degradation? What is Alice Walker, of all people--educated, sophisticated, militant, socially and politically active, author of The Color Purple--what is she doing, writing such a story? Is she flagellating herself through her portrait of Dee? (This might be a good time to try to distinguish the writer from the writing.)

What I think I will try if the discussion goes this way--and especially if it goes on too long--is to present the story stripped of race and ethnicity. Do the characters have to be black? Isn't this the story of down-home intelligence, warm emotions and sensibility, each honed by adversity, set off against the callowness of youth, the callousness of upward social mobility, and the conceit of education beyond your background? Do any of your students--white, yellow, red, brown, or whatever--recognize themselves in Dee? Do any wince at thinking of their first trip home after Psychology 101 and Art History 210 (not to mention English 101)? "Everyday use" can, it seems, be use of everyday intelligence, can be everyday values, can be the tried and the true, can be the useful versus the decorative. That the story circles--and also encircles--issues of race and heritage might, if we are lucky, come out in a spirited class discussion.

Gail Y. Miyasaki
OBACHAN

Short story; Japanese-American
This little narrative in many ways lies at the heart of a major issue in this chapter: the personal ties between family members separated by generations and cultures but tied together by deep love. The narrator's love for her grandmother is presented tenderly and indirectly but deeply and movingly, something you may need to work on a bit in class--the soft, subtle tone sometimes escapes readers. (To bring this to the surface is the point of the first study questions, you will have noticed.) The cultural gulf between them first surfaces with the kimono but appears most clearly in the story of the narrator's Aunt Mary. Here again is indirection: the narrator never openly states her feelings about Mary's marrying a Caucasian sailor, but we can understand, it seems to me, her responses through her mother's.

This combination of love and cultural difference is encapsulated in the title, the Japanese word for "grandmother," both loving and, for English-speaking Americans like the narrator, "foreign." This "encapsulation," the fusing of meanings that can be separated out but not wholly paraphrased without

sacrificing affective weight, is what I most often point
to when I use the word "symbol."


Paula Gunn Allen
GRANDMOTHER

Poem; Native American (Sioux-Laguna) and Lebanese-Jewish
     Speaking of "symbol," as I was doing at the end of
the "Obachan" comments, here is a symbolic poem as I
understand it. Perhaps you can paraphrase the weaving as
"creation," or, more specifically, "creation of life."
But you cannot then substitute that paraphrase for the
image of weaving as it weaves through the poem. Yet it is
meaningful. This is a complex and crucial issue and this
may be a good hook to hang the discussion on, for it is
both moving (isn't it? you might ask the class first for
affective responses to the poem) and, in its fashion,
"clear"--that is, the "gist" seems clear. So I like--
uncharacteristically--to begin here with the "gist."
Few of my students fail to feel they know what the poem
"means." Then I ask them to paraphrase the details, the
lines or phrases one by one. When a problem arises I ask
how you can understand the poem but not its details.
(Note that in the third study question I am reduced to
saying "apparently.") And off we go . . .


Pam Durban
ALL SET ABOUT WITH FEVER TREES

Short story; Regional
     Do we, as teachers, admit in our secret hearts that
we do, despite all our strivings, sometimes have "pets"?
Well, anthologists--I hate to admit--do, too. This is one
of my pets, one of the pieces I am most pleased to have
"discovered" in preparing this volume. (Not that I
discovered it, any more than Columbus discovered America,
but the "natives" at the Georgia Review who first
published it and those who awarded it a Pushcart Prize do
not count. I, I believe, discovered it for the great
world of anthologies.) Perhaps because it is a favorite, I
am not able to be very helpful in suggesting ways in
which it might be presented in class. (It is also a
handicap that I am just now, as the volume is going to
press, getting ready to teach it for the first time.) But
can't you just see what a wonderful story it is? And
surely your students can, can't they?
     Of course one of the qualities of a fine literary
work is its irreducibility, the relation of everything in
it to everything else, so it is difficult to pull one
passage or element out and say this is what makes the
story special. But I'll try. (This is not so much to

convince you--because of course, <u>you</u> will recognize the quality of the story immediately, but to perhaps help you to explain to your class why you feel the way you do about it. At least that's my excuse; you'll want to pick your own passage.)

So I look at paragraphs 51 and 52, for example. There is the sensory image in the second sentence, for example--the clammy quilt against the skin--and there is the graphic realization of Annie's movement, standing up "as if I'd remembered someplace I had to go." This particularization of place, action, and feeling pervades the paragraph in the way she smokes the cigarette, in the way she stares at the rhododendron flower, and in the vivid details of what she imagines, and in the last sentence of the paragraph ending on the crescendo of "pure life."

The passage, in addition, recaptures aspects of childhood in a profoundly original manner. I see this originality not just in the perfectly natural snitching of the cigarette hidden in the waistband of Annie's shorts and the adolescent's solitary communing with the sky and nature--so reminiscent of Thomas Wolfe--but in the belief in and expectation of "special powers," the ability "to penetrate the layer of troubles that seemed to lie over everything like humid heat over Macon" (and oh, yes, the perfect, sensory simile). Annie applies beautifully her gift of "special powers" to her adolescent sense of separateness, her realization of the difficulty of understanding reality and others, her yearning to find true peers, her ache to feel somehow special or superior, and on her desire to "do good": "I imagined myself going back to school with these special powers, able to tell who my real friends were and my secret enemies, able to know the secrets people keep in their hearts and to help them with their darkest troubles."

One of the virtues of the story, for me, is the risk it takes in trying to bring together so much, so many of the members of the family, from grandmother to mother to aunt, and their potentially separate stories. This may be where those not as enamored of the story as I may point out their reservations. I think it succeeds triumphantly. We may have trouble, however, countering the student who says that it "rambles on," goes from one story (the grandmother) to another (the aunt) and covers too much time to achieve the sense of concentration that a short story "must" have (says who?). I guess I just think stories that open out, that are centrifugal, are better, other things being equal, than those that are spare and tightly organized and controlled and centripetal.

Yvonne Sapia
GRANDMOTHER, A CARIBBEAN INDIAN, DESCRIBED BY MY FATHER

Poem; Puerto Rican-American
There seems to me a remarkable amount of detail
about the life of the grandmother not too deeply embedded
in this relatively brief poem.  It begs to be the center
of a writing assignment in which students reconstruct,
either in a prose narrative or in a descriptive essay,
the grandmother's life.
What students may miss is the affective power of the
poem. Though it seems to many on first reading rather
matter-of-fact (which may tell us something about the
speaker within the poem, the father), it is very moving,
and you may want to ask your students to look at the poem
more carefully to determine why that is so. You may begin
by asking them to notice all the words and phrases that
have to do with feelings, like "grieve," and "broke . . .
like hearts" in the first verse-paragraph. Then you might
ask them to pick out all the negatives suggesting
deprivation: "no map," "never young," "no wings," and so
on.
I like to give some attention to the speaker,
inferring both from the tone and language and from some
of the details--no room for him, he hoped there would be
room in New York, his mother did not come to the pier to
see him off, etc.--what his life was like, what his
relationship to his mother was like, and what emotions,
like love and regret the poem suggests on his part.
I imagine you could then come full circle and try to
define what the poet's view or feelings (or those of the
first-person [my] in the title) about the father are, but
I have not yet come to that in class.


Barbara Watkins
JOSEFA KANKOVSKA


Poem; Czechoslovakian-American
Like the Rhoda Schwartz poem in the previous chapter
and the Linda Pastan poem later in this chapter, a
photograph is an important element in this poem. (Why do
so many poems of Eastern European forebears and poems by
women of that heritage feature photographs so
prominently? coincidence? the editors' unconscious
intention?) Another poem with which this might be
compared is Irving Layton's "Keine Lazarovitch,"
especially in its ll. 18 and 23--"the distrust of people"
and "carrying her closed face like a fist," for example--
though here the love of the speaker comes through a bit
more obviously and the character who gives her name to
the title comes through a little less clearly.

Joseph Bruchac
ELLIS ISLAND

Poem; Slovak and Native American (Abnaki)
We almost put this poem in chapter 8, "Crossing,"
because, like "Song of the Breed" and "Flipochinos" there,
it concerns the offspring of a "mixed" marriage (see
also the comments on Tony Ardizzone"s "My Mother's
Stories," chapter 2.) The focus here, however, is on the
Slovak grandparents and their forebears for "a thousand
years" and on the Native American forebears back before
Columbus "discovered" America.

The first two paragraphs particularize the
conventional version of the American dream: poor
immigrants who come to this country to "make something of
themselves," to own property, line 13 seems to suggest.
And the second verse-paragraphs reinforces and
generalizes this dream--for ninety years Ellis Island has
received such immigrants.

The shift comes in the final verse-paragraph. The
speaker's other heritage is Native American, and theirs
is not the American Dream but the American Reality, at
least the Reality That Was, a culture in which land was
not owned, whose land and whose dream was invaded.

Of course the immigrants are not the invaders. Or
are they? This, once the details of the poem are
discussed, is where class discussion ought really to get
going. We all decry the cruelties of Cortez and the death
march of the Cherokees, but to what extent are the rest
of us--those non-Native Americans whose families came as
poor immigrants seeking freedom and opportunity--
accessories after the fact, benefiting from injustices
that we did not "personally" commit, that, more than
likely, our own forebears did not commit? What, then, do
we "owe" to Native Americans? Should we sell Manhattan
back for some beads? cede all property? settle somehow?
if so, how?

This issue can of course also be expanded to include
slavery and what white Americans owe to those who helped
build the country while in bondage and did not profit
from their toil. And it can also cross our boundaries and
oceans--why was not all the property the Nazis
confiscated from Jews returned after World War II, if not
to the original owners, most of whom were killed, at
least to the Jewish community? And in a slightly
different issue, where do you start--or stop--the
historical clock to decide "property rights"? Who lived
in Palestine--in 1947, 1897, 33 A.D., 2000 B.C.?

R. T. Smith
YONOSA HOUSE

Poem; Native American (Tuscarora)
In our "youth is beautiful" culture, we may need to
ask why this poem lingers on or at least specifies so many
"unattractive" physical details about the grandmother
(and perhaps ask students to list these details). This may
lead to a discussion of how "heritage" as a topic really
has to do with respect, even reverence, for the past and
thus for the aged or aging. (Most of the works in the
chapter are about grandfathers and grandmothers, the
living part of the older heritage.) This is a
particularly good poem to use as the center of such a
discussion, it seems to me, because we can also bring up
the unyielding attitude of the grandmother, her stubborn
alliance with the tradition; her apparent refusal to be
buried in a Baptist cemetery, for example. This may be a
good occasion, too, to ask that students look at the
pieces in the chapter not only in terms of how much the
heritage is revered and regretted but also how much the
"new ways" are also praised or admired or preferred.
Here, for example, nothing seems to exist of the conflict
between loyalty to the heritage and living in the modern
world.
This may lead the discussion into the tone, or into
how the love of the speaker for his grandmother is
expressed. Why, you might ask, is it her hands that he
thanks in l. 34? This question will take you back to l. 1
and ll. 20-23. You might ask, too, how his carving the
coffin lid pays tribute to what he got from his
grandmother.


Michael Harper
GRANDFATHER

Poem; Afro-American
My students have great difficulty with this poem--
and I have a little myself. That the film The Birth of a
Nation incited the neighbors of the speaker's grandfather
to burn down the grandfather's house as a gesture meant
to help found the Great White Nation is clear enough, I
suppose. Playing the film backwards on the speaker's eyes
(ll. 46-47) is a different story. As I read it, the film
is not literally run backwards from the rescue of the
white ladies by the KKK, but the racial theme is
reversed--the speaker is tempted to violence to found a
Great Black Nation. I am not sure of this, and not all my
students agree--with me or with each other. You might
want to try it out on your class. (And let me know what
happens.)

This crux, though, gives me a chance to talk about communication, especially in poetry, beyond or outside the normative semantic lexicon and syntactic structures. My class tends to agree, for example, that besides indignation at the event or near-event of 1915 and the admiration for the grandfather, there is something "strong" being said here, whether it is a threat of violence, just militancy without specific violence, or even a determination not to endure racial injustice any longer. Perhaps the strength of the poem lies in the reader's inability to pin down precisely what is being said--or threatened: it may become stronger and more menacing as it stands.

I'm uncomfortable condoning or praising uncertainty or ambiguity (as opposed to ambivalence), so I usually return to safer ground and point out that sometimes mere juxtaposition outside syntax communicates a meaning beyond the statement. And I fall back on "classics" like Wordsworth's Westminster Bridge sonnet--"Never did sun more beautifully steep / In his first splendour, valley, rock, or hill;"--where "steep" clearly means "soak" but where its proximity to valley and hill adds the other meaning of "steep."

Alberto Ríos
MI ABUELO

Poem; Chicano

My students take to the fantasy here more readily than I, in my old-fashioned way, do. Not that I don't like this poem immensely, or find it both moving and amusing, but my pedestrianly realistic soul says, "Well, it is moving and amusing, but is it really serious literature, what with dead grandfathers predicting the future through pipes leading from where he is buried to the surface? Where is Matthew Arnold now that we need him?" But I'm tickled and admiring despite myself. (Maybe you will have some old-fashioned students: eighteen year-old sometimes are more reactionary and "older" than those ten, twenty, even fifty years older than they. Unless you have offended the academic gods, however, you won't have a whole class full of them, and their peers should bring them kicking and screaming into the final decades of the twentieth century. Anyway, the reactionary line is worth a try, if only to get things stirred up. I find, much to my chagrin, that it is easier to get my classes to talk when they want to disagree with me than when we all agree about the work at hand.)

Some of the apparently fantastic lines seem metaphors (or is that just my Victorianism coming out?): e.g., that the grandfather speaks through all the mouths in the house (ll. 9-10) suggests to me, especially in the context of this chapter, that the family has been influenced by the grandfather, that he has passed on the heritage to the family, etc.

The earlier life of the grandfather is here hinted at and can be reconstructed, though perhaps not in so much detail as that of Sapia's Caribbean grandmother in the earlier poem. It might be fun to suggest that students try to imagine this grandfather and that grandmother meeting (in the afterlife, perhaps).

Linda Pastan
GRUDNOW

Poem; Polish-American
I love the first three lines of this poem, and, ham that I am, like to say "Grudnow" as I imagine the grandfather said it, pronouncing the "w" as a "v," of course. I try to make the hamming relevant by asking the class to look at the other figures of speech in the poem that fuse or juxtapose the historical or political with the private and personal: the shaky hand drawing the border between Russia and Poland and the long history of that border being "adjusted" (or erased) time and again; the Jews--I presume--digging in their heels (I suppose during the Holocaust) as hard as the heels of the grandfather's bread, and others.

I use this poem, sometimes, to get into the subject of "word-play" or form and its relation to meaning or theme. Here, for example, I ask if these figures are just verbal pyrotechnics, brilliant displays of verbal wit, or a keen eye for similarities. Does anyone, I ask, see any deeper relevance to the fusions or juxtapositions? Sometimes I'm lucky, and I get a groping toward the implication in the poem that our lives are lived in a context both as small as our kitchen table and as large as world conflict, and that public events, migrations, conflicts, are made up of and are influenced by the same elements and people that make up the family photographs and the group around the table.

But I do not like to leave this poem before someone points out that the speaker is alive only because of the migration and the resistance. She owes her life to the decisions and struggles and strength of those who came before. Don't we all. This is a tribute to our forebears and heritage.

Is there a little sense of "survivor's guilt" here? or "there but for the grace of God go I"? Do you have students who are benefiting from the sacrifices of their parents and grandparents? Are you?

Maxine Hong Kingston
NO NAME WOMAN

Narrative; Chinese-American
One of the aims of this anthology was to offer
pieces seldom if ever anthologized, and, even when the
authors were "canonized," the pieces chosen were not. But
Kingston is perhaps the only Asian-American "in the
canon," and this is undoubtedly her most anthologized
piece. We were almost obligated to include this rather
familiar piece because, besides our own desire to be
inconsistent and avoid being accused of having petty
minds, it represents so graphically the issues and
origins of the noncanonical American literature that by
its significance and power is forcing its way into the
canon.
This is the story of leaving "home," some other land
and culture, coming to America, and in one, two, or three
generations making one's way with difficulty and regret,
weaving the old heritage and the new society together in
some way, loose or tight. That's why I start with the
last two sentences of paragraph 10: "Those in the
emigrant generations who could not reassert brute
survival died young and far from home. Those of us in the
first American generations have had to figure out how the
invisible world the emigrants built around our childhoods
fit in solid America." (I have used this passage as an
essay question on the final examination, asking students
to apply it to two short stories and two poems, or a
play, a story, a poem, depending on what we covered and
how long the answer is intended to be.)
When I begin with that passage, I sometimes go on to
par. 12, not so much to pursue Kingston's piece as to
discuss the general issue raised in that paragraph. A
British friend of mine once told me with glee that her
daughters, seven and nine, were ashamed of her. I didn't
understand. "Well," she said, "I walked them to school
this morning and they asked me not to go right down to
the school but to turn back at the corner." But I still
did not understand why she was glad. "Don't you see?" she
said, "I have always been a little ashamed of my parents.
And I thought it was a matter of class. I've been feeling
guilty all these years, me a socialist--and a snob. But,
you see, I just realized today that all children are
ashamed of their parents." Do your students feel that
way? Do they admit it? Many of mine don't, but most are
sons and daughters of the rich and successful. Is it
that, or is it a generational thing? Were kids a
generation or two ago more likely to be uneasy about
their parents?
I've allowed myself to get off the subject here
because I often allow my students to do the same and
sometimes that turns out to be one of the better classes

of the term (but sometimes it doesn't). So back, more or less, to the text.

Another reason I like this piece is that it challenges some of the conventional beliefs (which we think of as unconventional) of our time and culture. My classes (and I) are horrified by the cruel attack on the aunt by the villagers. So terrible a punishment for so trivial--and commonplace, and even "natural"--an offense (not sin, not crime)! Kingston points out in par. 15 that the conditions of life in the Chinese village made adultery a threat to the whole society but she does not condone the cruel conditions, the subjection of women. She merely tries to "place" them in the cultural context, to understand them. Nor does she spare women entirely-- the pains they went (go?) through out of vanity(?) are graphically, painfully detailed.

I don't always spend much time on the formal aspects of prose, but next time I teach this I think I'll work over par. 21 in class. The line and color here remind me of Chinese calligraphy or painting--"a few hairs, a line, a brightness . . . "--but of course she uses more than the static and the visual--"a soft voice or a slow walk . . . a sound, a pace . . . a pigtail that didn't toss when the wind died . . . ." And then the dying fall of the final sentence of that paragraph, making "the flesh" beautiful and compelling as it is, evanescent, "trivial": "Why, the wrong lighting could erase the dearest thing about him." I like to get the class to build up the catalogue of the sensory and sensual in this paragraph and then I ask them about the final two and a half sentences of the paragraph--giving up the family just for such easily erasable charm. That should set your class to rebelling.

But don't let them get away until you get to the effect of the aunt's story, and its suppression, on the speaker. Ask them to discuss that strong final paragraph. Ouch!


Peter Blue Cloud
TO-TA TI-OM (FOR AN AUNT)

Poem; Native American (Mohawk)
Like the speaker's grandmother in "Yonosa House," the aunt in this poem is not exactly Miss America. You may want to talk about beauty and affection, and, as in R. T. Smith's poem, the homage to the elderly in so many of these heritage pieces. You may also want to hark back to Linda Hogan's "Heritage" to ask about the association of the heritage and elderly Native American women and tobacco. (Of course, tobacco was one of the indigenous people's contributions to Europeans--or was it vengeance?)

Are any of your students offended by the implied preference of the poem for the pagan ways and the pagan aunt over the Christians who dismissed her and their children who feared her? I like to start an argument by asking whether the poem endorses (authorizes) the medicine doctoring and pagan ways or merely honors the (benighted but beloved) aunt. It seems ll. 36-40 hedge a bit, the roots having power for "those who had need of such strength." Does that mean the roots were for those who were ill or were they for those who believed in such medicine and thus "needed" it in order to feel better? Then, there's the fulfilled prediction of her death--prophecy or coincidence or mind over body?

## Michael Ondaatje
## LIGHT

Poem; Dutch-Sri Lankan-Canadian

Old photographs surface again (Rhoda Schwartz, Barbara Watkins, Linda Pastan), but this time not Eastern European or female.

For the purposes of the chapter, I stress the relationship of this poem to the other photograph poems, the speaker seeing his family and forebears in his own figure in the mirror (ll. 59-60) as Linda Hogan did in "Heritage," and the extravagant stories bordering on fantasy (almost as much as "Mi Abuelo"). In many ways it has it all (though there does not seem to be much cultural or cross-cultural conflict).

But then I like to get to the poem itself, starting, how unorthodox, with the first line--but not the first words. How do your students understand the "walking off" of the trees in "fury"? (Of course many will not have noticed that at all until you mention it, so you are asking a leading question--but what's a teacher for?) The answer is not clear until the final half-dozen lines of the poem--if then--when the speaker recognizes that the trees have not moved an inch. In other words, we need to discourage the responses to the first question that suggest it is "only a figure of speech"--it is, instead, a perception. There's lots about perception here--you might want to ask the class to dig it out, sooner or later getting to the title of the poem. You can play the game of naming how many kinds of light there are in the poem--lightning, candlelight, projector light, electric light . . . . Perhaps then they'll see the light?

William Saroyan
NAJARI LEVON'S OLD COUNTRY ADVICE TO THE
YOUNG AMERICANS ON HOW TO LIVE WITH A SNAKE

Short story; Armenian-American
The works by Pam Durban, Yvonne Sapia, and Maxine
Hong Kingston in this chapter, and Tony Ardizzone's "My
Mother's Stories" in chapter 2, as well as this Saroyan
story, all are in one way or another about telling
stories--how to do it, what they're for, what kind of
stories to tell. If your class is interested in writing,
even "creative" writing, you might want to stop at this
point and go back over all the works named and infer
directions and definitions.
Levon is telling the story in Armenian, and there is
a rhythm and pattern in the English prose of the story he
tells that suggests its "foreignness" (I cannot say
"Armenianness" since I don't know Armenian, but it does
sound a little like Fitzgerald's translation of <u>Omar
Khayyam</u> and a little like Kahlil Gibran, so maybe there
is a Middle Eastern sound). The long sentences made up of
added-on clauses, often independent clauses one after
the other (run-on sentences), the simple, direct
language, and the repetition no doubt have something to
do with it. (I use paragraph 30 to illustrate.) There is
something of the same rhythm in Saroyan's prose when it
is not imitating Levon as well (par. 1, for example).
This may be a good point to go back over some of the
other poems and stories and prose pieces your class has
read listening for *dialogism*, the sound of another
voice--another culture, in these pieces--infiltrating, as
it were, the English in which it is written. Don't you
find something "foreign," even "Eastern," in the poetic
language of Agha Shahid Ali? Is there not something
East Asian in the rhythms and structures of the poems of
Li-Young Lee? This is a difficult topic to discuss. If
you are very lucky you may have one or more students from
one or more of these cultures who could help define just
what it is we are hearing (or dispel the whole notion).
You may, if you are not Anglo-Saxon, be able to choose a
short piece out of your own heritage and demonstrate for
the class how what they are reading is a harmonic blend
of English and something else.
Snakes, of course, have had a bad press, and the
small green snake in par. 3 costs the player ten points,
which does not endear snakes much to the children playing
the game. So Levon's story seems to be about getting
along with others, so that "star" and snake by the end of
the story do not seem worth quarreling about. If your
class takes the lesson too much to heart, however, they
won't want to argue about the story. This might be the
time that you do what I try to do two or three times a
term, have the students read aloud, not just poems but

stories like this one. Once in a while, I find, my class
needs to coast. That, after all, is what literature is
all about, we keep telling ourselves--and others. Enjoy!

# 4
## TRIBE

Most of the selections in this chapter are about the
power of the tribe.  Sometimes an individual struggles
against that power, sometimes the struggle is simply to
understand the power and come to terms with it
practically.  Nearly all students will have experienced
some form of this struggle already, although it may have
been focused primarily in a relationship with a single
individual, a powerful father or mother, for example.  If
it has been focused in this way, you may need to help
them distinguish, for purposes of discussing the readings
in this chapter, between struggles against the "tribe"--
that is, against traditions, customs, and habits of a
national, ethnic, or racial group--and those against
figures of authority or those in some sort of special
competitive relationship.  The distinction is important
for the very first selection in this chapter, "Girl," in
which a powerful voice gives a series of commands and
put-downs to a young girl. The voice is, in one sense,
simply the mother's voice, but there are indications in
the voice's ritual repetition that it speaks for a whole
tradition of beliefs about children and parents.  Rather
than plunging straight into the story, a rather complex
one to sort out because of its unusual presentation of
the narrator, I suggest that you have your students do a
short written exercise, either as an assignment before
reading " Girl" or as an in-class exercise after they
have read the story but before discussing it.  The
exercise would be to remember and write down some moment
they recall from childhood in which someone--a parent,
grandparent, aunt or uncle, teacher, or some other
authority figure--chewed them out and belittled them.
Get them to record exact words, several sentences, if
possible; give them plenty of time (if you do it as an
in-class exercise) to remember how the moment felt and to
try to sort out silently how they now feel about it.
Then ask them to write a paragraph about the person who
spoke the words, trying to account for why he or she
spoke so sharply or belittlingly.  Where did the person's
anger come from?  Where did the words come from?  Did the
words sound as if they were being repeated or rehearsed,
as if they had been said earlier to someone else? You
might or might not, depending on how well you know the
class and how relaxed the students are with each other,
wish to have them discuss the "speech" and their response
to it before going on to discuss the reading.  Even
without any discussion of the exercise, however, the
students will be somewhat sensitized to the issues of
voice in "Girl," and you will have indirectly introduced
them to the issue of *focus* and *point of view* taken up at

the end of the chapter. You will then be able to begin
to introduce various questions about the narrator's
perspectives, values, and limits for any of the
selections in the chapter before addressing the issue
more fully and summarily later on.


## Jamaica Kincaid
## GIRL

Narrative; Caribbean (Antiguan)
     The study questions here point toward a class
discussion of the kinds of issues described above. You
may need to stop, early in the discussion, for several
minutes to sort out exactly just how much information we
are given about the girl and about the mother. How much
characterization do we get? How much particularity about
setting? about habits and rituals? It is also worth
spending time to sort out precisely what values the
mother thinks she is upholding in the speech and how,
according to her, behavior and values are linked. Another
interesting topic for discussion, or for a written
exercise, is the difference between oral and written
modes. Get your students to tell you how they can be
sure that the mother's harangue is spoken rather than
written. What features give it away? How would the same
content be delivered in written form? One exercise might
involve having someone just like the mother in the story
write a letter to someone just like the daughter.


## Muriel Rukeyser
## TO BE A JEW IN THE TWENTIETH CENTURY

Poem; Jewish-American
     You may not be teaching verse forms or literary
kinds in this course, and you may not wish to talk about
this poem as a sonnet. But even if you don't want to
name the form or discuss anything about the
characteristics, traditions, and expectations of such
"compacted" verse, you can do a useful exercise on the
general and the particular, showing how the first eight
lines of the poem relate to the last six.


## John Fante
## THE ODYSSEY OF A WOP

Short story; Italian-American
     It may be time to begin to highlight some questions
about language (which the next chapter will deal with
extensively). This selection and the next ("Our Tongue
Was Nahuatl") are good ones in which to begin to discuss

the kinds of power that language tends to assume in particular cultures. Here language is only one of several features Fante isolates as important to adolescents trying to establish themselves as independent human beings, even while they are still discovering features of their cultural identity. The power of words--especially derogatory words--to get emotional responses is worth exploring in detail in class, and you might wish to indulge some autobiographical anecdote-telling here, first to establish the point of how dependent people tend to be on external verification and on the language in which it is expressed, and second, to show how language is used to manipulate, on a very fundamental level, human response. You might want to point ahead here to the autobiographical essay by Gloria Naylor in the next chapter, or (conversely) to return to discuss the Fante selection further once you have the more theoretical essay by Naylor in front of the class. In any case, it is a good time to read the Naylor essay yourself: it will offer insights into this selection.

Another way to teach this selection, emphasizing the way character is revealed and the narrative structured, is suggested by the study questions. If you end up spending much of the class time on character revelation, you might still wish to suggest briefly how the narrator's developing sophistication about language helps to measure his understanding of himself and his culture.


Ana Castillo
OUR TONGUE WAS NAHUATL

Poem; Native American (Aztec)
The title here can generate a good discussion of how the poem works. Language is mentioned as a group feature in only a single line of the poem while other cultural features--religion, for example, and landscape and daily customs--are mentioned repeatedly. Why, then, does language become the distinguishing feature for the title? In what ways does language operate within the poem itself? How is recognition of likeness signalled in the poem? Why is the first sentence of the poem an entire sentence?

The study questions will prepare your students for a discussion of subservience and subordination, and you might want to help them see that the "bowing" imagery is set up by the prior discussion of religion and subservience to the divine. Have them discuss what kind of comment on the invaders can follow from the fact that they are structurally associated with that which is bowed down to.

Virginia Cerenio
[WE WHO CARRY THE ENDLESS SEASONS]

Poem; Filipino-American
     This poem recalls several of the selections in
chapters 2 and 3. You might wish to use this
opportunity to look back at poems or stories which,
although centered on a particular relative--mother,
father, aunt, etc.--present indirectly the legend of a
whole people.  Here, the powerful emphasis on how blood,
obligation, and custom inevitably affect character, even
across oceans, is illustrated by the insistent Filipino
phrases as well as the "natural" ties of childbirth.  Get
your students to discuss how the sense of inevitability
is communicated, how customs are made to seem to grow out
of biological and linguistic processes.
     One good way to get into the issues of this poem--
and thus to return to issues of parenthood and family
ties that you may have emphasized in earlier selections--
is to have the discussion isolate the key words this poem
uses, pitting events of a single instant (heartbeats,
breathing) against a sense of process, unvarying
repetition, and permanence (seasons, shadows, desires,
dreams, guilt).  Note how much the poem depends on the
single word "carry" in line 1, how crucial women are
biologically and emotionally to the process of passing on
customs and values.  Get the class discussion to isolate
the biological from the customary and both of the above
from individual acts.  How much room does the poem leave
for individual choice?  Contrast the sense of total
tribal control here with that in other selections (for
example, Woo's "Letter to Ma," Gilchrist's "Traveler"
or Silko's "Private Property") in which the need to
express individual difference from family and tribe is
asserted.


Marcela Christine Lucero-Trujillo
THE MUSICOS FROM CAPULIN

Poem; Chicana
     Contrast the images this poem uses to express
continuity with the past to those in the Cerenio poem
above. You can build a good class discussion comparing
the two poems on questions of effectiveness and value
(but be careful not to "put down" one poem in order to
elevate the other one). Ask your students to explain the
differences of organization and try to suggest why this
poem uses a single moment to recall a past while Cerenio
establishes process first and then moves to particulars
which are comprehended in the process. Get them to
discuss the implications of the different organizations
for the poems' effects.

Richard Olivas
[I'M SITTING IN MY HISTORY CLASS]

Poem; Chicano
    I like to get the students to talk fully about the
speaker here, what we know, what we don't know, how he
(is it a he?) is characterized.  This can lead to a good
discussion of why particular words are used, what levels
of language and what kind of humor are employed, and even
how the rhyme is used.  Get them to discuss what is
effective about the rhyme here and why it fits this
particular speaker.  Get them to talk about how the
repetition works here, how method reinforces content. If
you have taught the concept of tone in the previous
chapter, this is a good poem to use to reinforce the
discussion. You can get a lively debate going on the tone
here, especially on how to read the smart-alecky last
stanza (which, I think, has to be read in terms of the
external respect for authority--"Dare I ask . . ." and
the raising of the hand).  Ask them to show how the tone
moves the poem from jest to a serious questioning of what
American history consists in.  Then get them to show how
the gradual revelation of character leads to the same
place.


Toni Morrison
1920

Short story; Afro-American
    It may be well to begin the discussion of this story
by simply straightening out the characters and exactly
who they are, having the class describe as they go
exactly what we know about each person except Nel. I
suggest holding back a discussion of Nel until everyone
else is clarified; that can move you efficiently toward
issues of self-knowledge and identity which are central
to the story. The discussion of Nel needs to be quite
full, I think, to give everyone an opportunity to see how
her hopes and fears are gradually revealed. One way to
suggest some of Nel's complexity is to draw into the
discussion a reexamination of the issues in Cerenio's
poem above. Part of what makes Nel so fascinated by
her experiences in New Orleans has to do with worries
(expressed in the Cerenio poem as values) about inherited
traits and habits, expecially what daughters take from
their mothers. Once you have isolated most of Nel's
character, discuss the two mother-daughter relationships in the story and how each of them comments on the
other.

Ray A. Young Bear
IN THE FIRST PLACE OF MY LIFE

Poem; Native American (Mesquakie)
You might use the dream quality of the poem to
recall the dream near the end of the Cerenio poem and
then move into a discussion of how much the two poems are
determined by their choices of organization, imagery, and
even in theme by their respective interests in the male
and female blood lines.

Paula Gunn Allen
POWWOW 79, DURANGO

Poem; Native American
See if this poem reminds your students in any way of
the Olivas poem above. They will likely want to talk
about similarities between the rebelliousness of the
daughter here and the speaker in Olivas's poem, and I
would let them do so for a while before asking them to
talk about how the differences between the two characters
lead the poems to emphasize different things about
history. Because the central event here involves an
attempt to preserve history, indeed reproduce it, the
ritual is in many ways like the authoritative ritual of
the history class in Olivas, though here the daughter
rebels against quite a different set of assumptions and
values. Get a discussion going about the importance of
whose story it is: in this case are we more curious about
the daughter or the mother-speaker? How might the poem
be different if it were written from the daughter's
perspective?

Leslie Marmon Silko
PRIVATE PROPERTY

Short story; Native American (Laguna)
A class discussion of this story can go a long way
from an initial listing on the board of differences
between "old ways" and "new ways." Get the students to
line up characters as well as values and then to think
about what the fences are supposed to do, who wants them
and why. It is worth spending some class time here on
the power of community feeling, noting in what ways rumor
and oral tradition affect individuals and their ability
to function effectively. It is also profitable to
discuss the differences in attitudes here toward women
and men, sorting out exactly what roles in the community
are associated with each gender and how the author seems
to feel about roles more generally. This is a tricky
story for sorting out exactly how the author relates to

the themes she embodies, but for that very reason it can
be a valuable one for beginning to articulate issues of
how you know, or what in the story allows you to
conclude, anything about the characters beyond their
opinions alone.

Arthur Laurents
WEST SIDE STORY

Play; Puerto Rican-American and mixed
     It is possible to do lots of different things with
this play, for your students will likely find it (as mine
do) at once very familiar and very remote.  You may do
well to begin there, getting them at first to talk about
how the situation and characters here differ from
themselves and particularly from a similar dramatization
of conflicts and themes if the play were to be reset in
the present.  They will be articulate about differences,
but you may have to push them a bit to talk about
similarities and whether they identify at all with the
rituals and attitudes.  If you have the leisure, it is a
lot of fun to stop halfway through the discussion here
and get the class to read Romeo and Juliet, not just
because West Side Story alludes so comprehensively to
Shakespeare but because the students will recognize more
readily the similar theme in a different historical
context if you have more than one past to compare with
the present.  The 1950s, in case you hadn't thought
about it, will be ancient history to your students,
however recent and relevant the time may seem to you.
     It is tempting to use the film of West Side Story
here as a comparative text, and it may well be a good
idea. I prefer, however, to use a film of Romeo and
Juliet, especially because I never can find time to read
the text of Shakespeare in the midst of the discussion
here, and some Shakespearean context is useful to the
discussion--to make a larger point about allusion, to
show how issues both vary and stay the same over time and
cultures, and to provide some visual sense of how
conflict works when large numbers of people--standing for
whole families or nations--are involved.  I think the
visuality and theatricality in West Side Story are very
important to see and rather hard to get at from the text
(though you can do wonders here with exercises in class
on how to stage particular scenes), and one way to
highlight such issues is by drawing them away from this
text and substituting another.  Since I'm not especially
fond of the film version of West Side Story (in spite of
its success), I prefer to use another visual example, and
a film version of Shakespeare can thus serve multiple
purposes.

If you decide to skip films as a device for emphasizing visual and dramatic features, you can do a lot with in-class writing exercises. You could ask students to describe, in a paragraph, how they would dress a particular character, e.g., Officer Krupke, or how they would stage a particular scene (I choose a very short scene in which there is relatively little movement, so that the initial emphasis falls on the visual panorama and the way two or three characters display their character through physical interaction).  I like to follow up exercises of this sort with blackboard demonstrations.  I prefer to have a student, usually someone with a bit of stage experience, go to the board and "block" the action, getting as many students as possible involved in suggestions about movement and repeatedly calling attention to the overall visual effects of polarization.  I find that students like to become involved in a sense of how a play is realized on the stage, though they are often not at all good, at first, at connecting action and effect.


Francine du Plessix Gray<br>
TRIBE

Short story; French-American
      This is the most difficult story in the chapter (and one of the most complicated in the book) but the time you may have to devote to it in the classroom is well worth it.  The story presents a useful paradigm for the New World/Old World dichotomy so important to much American experience. In the uncertainties of the narrator--about her family, her heritage, her identity, her self--one can see the reflection of many other consciousnesses trying to sort out their relationship to a past that they neither belong to nor feel quite free from.
      Again (as I have suggested for several selections earlier in this chapter) it is probably well to begin with a character other than the narrator.  My candidate is Aunt Charlotte, who is such a stereotype of anti-American prejudices and naivetés that she usually gets the attention of almost all readers.  Get the class to detail her ignorance fact by fact and prejudice by prejudice, and get them to suggest how her utter confidence in herself and her utter provinciality are made to seem plausible, even consistent within terms of her character.  Then ask in what ways she "represents" the old world, how "typical" she is of Europeans portrayed in the story.  I then spend a lot of time on the narrator, tracing in detail what we learn about her and her feelings, how she differs from her family in such a way as to define "new world" characteristics.  Finally, I get the students to compare her to other heroes and

Tribe / 52

heroines of narratives we have read so far, and look at the way that her perspective (point of view, focus, voice) makes the story unfold.

The language of the story is worth some class time, too. A brief discussion of how language works in this story will set up some categories for discussion in the next chapter. The language of course reflects the educated and sophisticated character of the narrator, and the sheer amount of information, much of it referential detail about American history and civilization, can lead quickly to a sense of what issues are important to the story. The amount of <u>allusion</u> also suggests something about the type of reader expected to pick up this story, and the complication and formality of the dialogue tip off the complexity of the narrative structure and the depth of psychological probing.

If you do a "digression" on language, or on some other narrative element such as structure or plot, I suggest you return before the end of class to the issues of point of view, focus, and voice for a final emphasis. It is also not a bad idea to do a little reviewing of earlier narratives for comparison--not just the ones you may have taught in this chapter with an emphasis on this technical issue but earlier ones about which your students will now have something more to say.

# 5
## DANGER: FOREIGN TONGUE

The selections in this chapter make quite a few different points about language. You may wish to start fairly simple discussions of the difficulties of translation or ease of misunderstandings across linguistic and cultural borders. Or you may wish, depending on the level of your class, to get into much more sophisticated matters involving different notions of language. In either case, you will probably wish to read, before teaching the selections, the brief--but I hope suggestive--afterword to this chapter in which some contemporary ideas about language are translated into simple terms. I strongly urge that you emphasize, in teaching individual selections, not just the way language is talked <u>about</u> but the way it is <u>used</u>. Most of the selections throughout the book use language self-consciously and with great precision so that close analysis of individual words and of the grammar and syntax of each selection will pay teaching dividends. The selections in this chapter in particular are worth using class time to examine how individual words and phrases work to produce specific effects. If you have not been especially emphatic about language in teaching the earlier selections, it is a good strategy to go back over several selections discussed earlier and show that they, too, merit close attention. There are plenty of good candidates for such a reexamination: the stories by Bissoondath, Ardizzone, Bellow, Angelou, Durban, and Gray; the poems by Hirsch, Song, Agha, Erdrich, Cervantes, Lee, Baca, Sapia, Ríos; and the plays by Yamauchi or Hwang. I would be guided, though, by what was missing in previous discussions, going back to items where "larger considerations"--plot, character, setting-- had dominated the discussion. The virtue of going back over selections taught earlier, besides the fact that it provides a review and implicitly makes comparisons among different selections and genres, is that it suggests that individual works do not simply <u>illustrate</u> a single point but rather are available to questioning of several different kinds. Implicitly it says to students: any piece of writing, including your own, can be analyzed for its constituent parts.

Mark Singer
TYPICAL

Narrative; Chinese-Jewish-Japanese-American
    This selection is not quite a "news item" but it is
from a recent magazine. If you put your students on the
alert they will readily be able to come up with items
from newspapers and magazines about language-crossing in
everyday life.  I like to challenge students to come up
with a similar kind of anecdote from the public press,
and in the meanwhile like to get them to recall moments
they remember or have heard of in which similar comic (or
even tragic) interchanges occur among people who come to
a conversation from different heritages.  I like
exercises in "conversion" too--in which I ask students to
translate an episode like the one described in "Typical"
to a different tone or mode.  For example, get them to
retell this moment in terms of some colossal
misunderstanding that makes of the moment a very
different experience, with a different outcome, different
tonal effects, and that leads to a different narrative
mode.  This can be a good exercise in self-consciousness
and has the virtue of recalling issues of tone raised in
chapter 3.


Leo Rosten
DANGER: FOREIGN TONGUE

Narrative; Mixed
    I like to teach this essay (perhaps a little
perversely) as an exercise in analyzing the narrator.
This strategy has the effect of "sneaking up" on
questions of language, for much of the characterization
of the narrator is done through his own uses of language
to be self-consciously cute or self-congratulatory about
his humor and wit.  And it has the advantage, important
to the way I like to mix the selections generically and
modally, of raising a kind of question about essays which
is usually reserved for stories or other narratives.  In
my experience, present-day students often don't think the
narrator's pose is very funny; they sometimes find him
condescending (in spite of his attempt to pretend to be
condescending, a posture that implies that underneath he
is not), perhaps because they find the whole pretense of
using English as a norm so preposterous that they think
he must be secretly even more chauvinist than he pretends
to be.  In any case, the selection is a good one not only
for discussing how tone is (or is not) controlled, but
also for showing how applications of language, in a
selection that is primarily about language, work to build
a character than one can feel strongly about emotionally.

Students who do like this selection--and some do
like it a lot--will find other Rosten creations
(especially those involving the "education" of H\*Y\*M\*A\*N
K\*A\*P\*L\*A\*N) very entertaining.  Often it is a good idea,
I think, to offer students a bit of information (if you
have it handy; often we include some in the headnotes)
about other writings by the author they have been
discussing.  You have to play this by ear, of course;
sometimes they don't want to know.  But especially when
an author has a very distinctive voice or style, and when
students show a strong interest in a particular
selection, it is useful to remind them that the library
offers them infinite extensions of the textbook.


Noel Perrin
OLD MACBERLITZ HAD A FARM

Nonfiction; Mixed
     I personally like this selection a lot but find it
very hard to teach; maybe you will have suggestions or
anecdotes from your own classroom experience.  One
strategy that sometimes works is to follow up on the
discussion of Rosten by asking similar questions about
authorial stance and tone.  Another is to try an exercise
in having students try to record, in writing, sounds they
have never seen spelled before: in my experience, city
sounds work best.  Make up the exercise yourself, and if
you have a varied class of students from different
cultures and linguistic backgrounds, you will be able to
do your own MacBerlitz experiment. Different people will
describe quite differently sounds that they may think
they hear alike.  In any case, a city version of farm
sounds can have an interest in itself for urban students
(who, these days, often think traditional writing is too
much about "nature," a nature many of them have never
encountered), and an exercise which demonstrates how
arbitrary written letters are as symbols for sounds can
be something of an eye opener to students who may find
the Perrin essay a bit unbelievable at first.


Gloria Naylor
MOMMY, WHAT DOES "NIGGER" MEAN?

Nonfiction; Afro-American
     Things to argue about in class: the power of the
written versus the spoken word (especially if you have
emphasized the arbitrariness of written representation of
sounds in the Perrin selection above), the power of a
label over a sense of self-identity (going back to the
Fante story can be useful), the way people read tone at
different ages or at different stages in their lives, and

the power of context over meaning. Almost anything works to get a good discussion going here, and your job may be to referee among personal anecdotes. Personal autobiography--told anecdotes or written assignments--can be usefully employed to personalize Naylor's point about how culture controls meaning and effect. I think it is worth spending a fair amount of class time on the implications of this point because students who have not thought a lot about language (or who have not yet had formal courses in language) often think of it as a "natural" phenomenon in which a word is almost an extension of the thing it tries to represent. Especially in a course in which cultural collisions are often signalled by different language representations, a sense of how language depends on communal agreement will be useful for several readings later in the course.

### Mary TallMountain
### THERE IS NO WORD FOR GOODBYE

Poem; Native American (Athabaskan)
Again here it is not a bad idea to work back toward personal experience or to move beyond the text by getting students to list words that literally mean the same thing as "goodbye" but which imply different things. Localisms may be interesting here as well as variations from language to language that your students may have in their backgrounds. Even if all your students are Anglo and homogeneous--from a similar place and social group-- you can raise their consciousnesses about connotation, tone, and implication by getting them to sort out what is "meant" by differences among "synonyms" like "so long," "see you later," "farewell," "ta-ta," "bye-bye," etc. Then get them to talk about what the lack of a word for goodbye implies about the culture's beliefs as represented in the poem. Make them back up their sense of implication from the text itself. How much does the poem tell us about Athabaskan belief systems?

### Sherley Williams
### THE COLLATERAL ADJECTIVE

Poem; Afro-American
If my experience holds true for your class, no one (or at least few students) will have thought to look up the word "collateral"--and the study questions here don't invite them to. Ask them what they <u>think</u> it means, and speculate about the disjunctions the poem expresses. Move toward pinning something down. <u>Then</u> go to a discussion of the speaker and the larger implications of form and pattern that the study questions lead to.

Lorna Dee Cervantes
REFUGEE SHIP

Poem; Chicana
I like to work out of the implications of a single
word, the word "refugee." Get your students to talk
about what refugee implies, and how it relates to
language deprivation. This is a good place to go back to
selections in chapter 1 and review some of the factors
involved in definitions of "home." It may well be that
language had not seemed to have been an important factor
in definition when they first discussed some of the
stories and poems there, and they should now be prepared
to think about a fuller cultural definition that includes
language as a crucial component. I try to do this by
concentrating on a single selection, sometimes deciding
which one by asking them what definitions of "home" they
remember in which language was omitted. Surprise them by
showing how matters of language were involved but not
articulated in, for example, the stories by Anthony and
Gilchrist or the poems by Cervantes or Lorde.


Richard Rodriguez
ARIA: A MEMOIR OF A BILINGUAL CHILDHOOD

Nonfiction; Chicano
Students will want to argue, many of them against
Rodriguez, about the advisability of bilingual education.
If you want them to understand Rodriguez's ideas about
"private" and "public" language, you will need to clarify
these ideas before opinions polarize too strongly about
educational philosophy. I like to start the discussion
far away from the theoretical, philosophical, and
educational issues which are ultimately likely to take
over the class; one way is to get students to concentrate
initially on how Rodriguez chooses to present himself,
how he uses language to influence the reader's _feelings_
toward him as a child and adult.
It is crucial to straighten out terminology early
(because Rodriguez uses and reuses several terms that are
important to his argument) if students are to respond to
Rodriguez's arguments instead of parody them. I get
students to put key terms on the board, just as they
would if they were analyzing an argument in philosophy,
and try to arrive at definitions from the text. The study
questions will set up the discussion: it may be time-
consuming, and you may need (surprisingly, I think) more
than a single hour on this piece.

Rita Dove
PARSLEY

Poem; Afro-American, Chicana
   This is not only a lovely poem but a powerful one,
satisfying formally (I find) besides being politically
provocative and useful for illustrating the cultural
barriers of language.  I like to start with the visual
qualities here, getting students to suggest how setting
and detail lead to emotional responses to the "two"
worlds.  Get them to see which words are especially
loaded; it is worth some class time to emphasize which
words are especially effective for the poet (who in this
authoritative respect is like "El General").  You can
also use this selection to make some distinctions about
modes; have them, for example, rewrite the poem into a
story and get them to analyze what they have to add to
make it work.  (Or you can do this hypothetically.  Or
you can have them take a story they have already read--
Fante's, for example, or Morrison's--and write it as a
poem in imitation of this one.)


Louise Erdrich
JACKLIGHT

Poem; Native American (Chippewa)
   This is a good poem from which to launch a
discussion, harking back to the Mary TallMountain poem,
of whether economy of words involves poverty or richness
in language.  I like to work from the epigraph (the study
questions will help set up the discussion), and go back
to other selections in which the ambiguity of a
particular word was crucial.  Let them suggest examples,
then have one ready that you want to return to in detail
(have your rationale ready for the importance of the
particular selection you feel is best).  Get them to draw
out the implications of the ambiguity, and make them
defend the significance of it by close references to the
text.
   Again here, as in the poem just preceding, a sort of
story is told, and again you may wish to make comparisons
with other poems and stories.  The isolation of the "we"
seems to me crucial to the effect here, and you may need
to spend some class time clarifying how sympathy is
channeled by the way the poem begins.


Salli Benedict
TAHOTAHONTANEKENTSERATKERONTAKWENHAKIE

Short story; Native American (Mohawk)
   I find this selection compelling to read, difficult

to teach.  The key to teaching it well is, I think, to
get the students to talk about, from the very start, what
kind of language the story uses.  Get them to make
comparisons with other things they have read.  Then get
them to characterize the world underlined_portrayed in the story and
ask them how language works in underlined_that world. Then get them
to talk about structure and outcome.  What do they miss
most?  In what ways does the story violate the normal
expectations of a short story?  What compensations does
it offer?  The point of having the story in a course, it
seems to me, is to suggest the value of labeling and the
role of language in setting expectations for readers.


Linda Hogan
SONG FOR MY NAME

Poem; Native American (Chickasaw)
      This poem can readily launch, quite beyond an
analysis of how the poem itself works, a discussion of
how names operate in life and in literature.  It is
useful, I think, to recall some of the "fictional" names
provided by authors in poems, stories, and plays already
read (I'd purposely leave out autobiographies and essays
which claim a different representational relationship),
and spend time on how the names worked to create
particular kinds of expectations.  Then move to "real"
names or the names that claim to be real in "non-
fictional" works:  what claims do these names make about
their significance in some larger world?  In what ways do
"works of art" imitate beliefs about the significance of
names in the real world?
      Get your students to talk about what "real" names
have caught their attention and what they feel is implied
by the names.  Get them to talk about the meanings of
their own names, both given and family, and find out what
range of self-consciousness you have represented in class
about name traditions and choices.  You may discover some
interesting variations of pattern among different
cultures represented in your class, and it may be worth
moving toward a research project--or series of projects--
on how different nations and cultures regard the process
of naming.  Hogan's poem obviously represents an extreme
of awareness of meanings not often duplicated in larger
cultures.


Nora Dauenhauer
TLINGIT CONCRETE POEM

Poem; Native American (Tlingit)
      My students love this poem, right down to its
allusive and mythic mechanisms. It can be hard to get a

discussion going, though, because there is no discourse or sequence here that readily leads to systematic discussion. I simply invite my students to make whatever observations they _feel_ like making. What do they see? What makes them think it means _anything_? What do words or language have to do with anything? Does the vocabulary of the visual arts offer any help in talking about the poem? I go out of my way to allow the discussion to wander here and not force too systematic an interpretion. Your students may volunteer some distinctions between kinds of poems if you ask them in what ways this poem is like, or unlike, other poems—and why.

## Li-Young Lee
## PERSIMMONS

Poem; Chinese-American

This incredibly sensual poem can be taught successfully in all kinds of ways because it is at once complex in its mechanisms and clear in its effects. I start with speaker and ask how attitudes toward him are developed, then ask toward what other persons or events they come to feel strongly. This method usually leads to the isolation of individual words and phrases that generate discussion and often argument. The study questions will readily lead you from individual words to larger patterns of voice and language.

Two poems by Li-Young Lee appear earlier (in chapter 2). If you have already taught them, it may be worthwhile to return to them here to notice what distinctive uses of language your students find in poems by the same author. You can also readily begin to ask evaluative questions out of this direction of discussion. Ask your students which of the poems they like best and why. The discussion can easily become enormously enlarged to include similar poems by other poets. If you introduce this issue, be prepared to limit—or divert or abort—the discussion if it becomes too general and unfocused.

## Pat Mora
## BORDERS

Poem; Chicana

Again here I like to work from the epigraph (almost always a good place to begin when writers bother to provide one). Get your students to define what "different languages" in the Gilligan quotation means (it will mean, by this point in the chapter, something much more sophisticated and flexible than it would have meant

earlier). What does the title mean? What are the
ironies of the frequent uses of "we," "our," and "us"?
The study questions here should provide your students
with plenty of material to bring to class. I would make
a point of specifically assigning the questions here with
the poem. Letting the discussion grow directly out of
their answers is a good strategy.


Maya Angelou
THE LANGUAGES OF HOME

Narrative; Afro-American
     Regional and racial "languages" here are more or
less equivalent to the languages of gender in the
preceding poem, but I tend to begin class discussion out
of traditional narrative categories: plot, character,
setting, structure. It turns out that all these
categories--almost automatically in the context of this
chapter--raise questions of how language is used to
clarify how they work. Get your students to detail how
language differs from person to person and group to
group. How many different languages can they
specifically identify in the story? The study questions
will lead your students to questions of how language
embodies values; many selections can be used to make the
same point, but the Angelou selection works especially
well. Although the story is quite subtle, the values are
easy to clarify in relation to individual characters.
The discussion here can be quite deep and quite long: if
you want to use part of the hour for other matters, you
will need to be prepared to cut the discussion of values
short.


Toshio Mori
JAPANESE HAMLET

Short story; Japanese-American
     This story seems to me very touching, and I like to
discuss it in terms of how attitudes are devloped toward
Tom. Students, however, often find it less affecting
than I do, and when they do I like to use their responses
as a way of exploring values prior to language. Why do
they become impatient with Tom before the narrator does,
long before I do? What predispositions do they recognize
in themselves? How does language control predispositions? What limits does language have over the givens
in readers?
     It is often useful to have students recall exactly
what the plot is here. What happens? Why does so little
happen? Why do we spend so much time on the narrator's

reactions? The study questions here will readily lead to class discussions of theme, character, and allusion.

## James Alan McPherson
## I AM AN AMERICAN

Short story; Afro-American and mixed

Try teaching this story first as an unfolding mystery, and get your students to detail exactly how things are revealed and held back. Then move to the character dimension, and lead the discussion to considerations of how uses of language, especially by Leroy, lead to judgments. So many stereotypes appear here that they force themselves into the discussion. Try to get fairly quickly to the self-conscious qualities of Leroy, his self-deprecation, his self-humor, his sense of his own awkwardness and limitations of perception. Steer the discussion ultimately toward questions--the study questions in the textbook will help set this up--about how we as readers sort among the stereotypes and choose someone to sympathize with.

## Israel Horovitz
## THE INDIAN WANTS THE BRONX

Play; Mixed

So many different languages come up here--and are staged quite theatrically--that this play can provide an easy summary of the issues of language illustrated throughout the chapter. I like to concentrate however, on a language used fairly distinctively here; the language of physical violence. If you have taught West Side Story, you will have at your disposal an interesting contrast. In West Side Story the violence seldom becomes language, even though the violence is ritualistic, because individual characters do not use it to express anything very important about themselves either as individuals or as members of a group. Here, however, all the rituals of violence express something quite specific. It is worth spending a fair amount of class time to have your students articulate exactly what it is that gets "expressed" by the different acts of violence--from horseplay, to "verbal" abuse of Gupta and the women who do not appear on stage, to the hurting of Gupta, and the breaking of communication by cutting the phone line. I like to get students to talk extensively about how the physical action reflects inner states, what the action tells us about Joey and Murph. I spend a lot of time on Joey and Murph, getting the class to detail exactly how they feel about them collectively and singly.

Staging is important here. If you have had students do exercises earlier on how they would stage a particular scene or set of moments in another play, it is worth following up here by having them consider how they would create effects based on characters who are important but don't appear, for example, the two women and Gupta's son. Get your students to discuss, as well, how a "majority" sense is created theatrically--by intimidation? by the physical appearance of the two boys? by the way language is used?

The study questions here will raise so many issues for class that you may need to assign them selectively depending on how much time you have to devote to the play and how you wish to focus the discussion.

# 6
## THE MAN FROM MARS

### Diane Burns
### SURE YOU CAN ASK ME A PERSONAL QUESTION

Poem; Native American (Ojibwa/Cheemehuevi)
This poem just cries out for a writing assignment that creates the other side of the conversation, either in dialogue, as in the poem (thereby making a brief play or dramatic skit), or in narrative, complete with descriptions of both speakers and perhaps even one or more settings. Imagining the other side of what lines 43, 45, 47, 49, and 59-61 are responding to may be particularly challenging and amusing.
If you don't have the time or the occasion, you could ask for extemporaneous responses in class. Another classroom possibility is asking various students to read the poem aloud or several students to read the same passages and discuss the possible differences in tone. The last two lines should generate some chuckles as students compete to see who can be grumpiest or most disgusted.

### Mitsuye Yamada
### LOOKING OUT

Poem; Japanese-American
This incisive little poem is also a profitable one to read aloud and to center a discussion of tone on. But I also like to use it as a portable, succinct example of how literature often leads, urges, or forces us to leave our own selves, our own pair of eyes, and imagine ourselves "over there," looking out from other eyes toward ourselves. To me, this is the moral as well as the aesthetic center of the literary experience.

### Tess Slesinger
### WHITE ON BLACK

Short story; White-black
You may have to warn (or inform) your students that when this story was written, over half a century ago, the term "Negro" was the acceptable term, the equivalent of "black" nowadays. I like to emphasize the relative hoariness of this story because it may seem to many so "modern." Is the fact that it seems new, I ask, good or bad? (A not very elegant way of asking the question.) Most of the time students will take the bait and declare

that it is good, that stories that seem timeless or
modern show the universality of art and all that. There
are always those, bless them, that see the hook: "It may
be good for the story," they say, "but it isn't very good
for black Americans [or "us," depending who is speaking]
that after the Movement and the Civil Rights laws and all
that has been done to improve 'race relations,' that even
now, almost three generations later, what happens in the
story, with very little change, can be seen as happening
here and now."

The "here" raises another issue or aspect, however.
The school in the story is private (and wealthy),
Northern, and genteel. How many of your students went to
such a school--or a comparable one? If any did, or if you
or they know someone well who did, recently, perhaps it
would be worthwhile to continue the discussion of the
here and now (or there and now) and discover how much
things have changed in such schools.

This is also a useful story, I find, with which to
analyze and discuss racism. This is surely a topic that
will come up in one form or another at one point or
another involving one race or ethnic group or another in
using this anthology. You may be able to use this story to
define a whole spectrum of racism or racial relations--
from deep personal distaste, through peer pressure and
personal cowardice, parental or authority pressures,
custom, and so on--and illuminate how racism influences
the behavior and attitudes of those who are discriminated
against--from self-hatred or self-deprecation to
defiance.


                    Marcela Christine Lucero-Trujillo
                      ROSEVILLE, MINN., U.S.A.

Poem; Chicana
        I like to play with the particulars of this wry
poem. I start with the "subjects," like who is the "one"
who notices in the first line, and who is the implied
[you] of the imperatives in lines 6, 7, 8? The grammar, I
try to point out, puts the reader in the position of the
chicano/a, a compadre of the speaker. The near
juxtaposition of "abuela," suggestive of her chicana
heritage, and the "culmination / of her cultural
perpetuation," measures semantically how far the speaker
has come (for better or worse). And there's the twist, of
course, of the grandmother being unhappy that her
granddaughter, who has moved out into American society,
should still be looking for the food of her oppression,
tortillas. Then I ask what it could mean that the
Southwestern chicano world and the Roseville gringo world
are not just different cultures or even worlds, but

different "realities." (Sometimes an alert student will
tie this into the Man from Mars motif of the chapter.)
   Otherwise, I approach this as a poem comparable to
"Sure You Can Ask Me a Personal Question," and I ask the
same question of the class that I do when I teach Diane
Burns' poem: "What stereotypes do the questions the
speaker is asked suggest?" Or, I ask them to compare the
questions and answers and the implied stereotypes in the
two poems.


                    Jack G. Shaheen
         THE MEDIA'S IMAGE OF THE ARABS

Nonfiction; Arab-American
   A dirty way to start talking about this article is
to ask the class to write down the names of the "21 Arab
nations" and of the two with which we are not on friendly
terms. I call the exercise "dirty" because I cannot do
it. To begin with, I don't think of Lebanon, the homeland
of Shaheen's parents, as Arab, somehow. Why? Do I think of
it as French? Or am I confused because of the strong
Christian population? And I'm a little confused by his
umbrage at the evil "Shiek Ha-Mean-Ie": isn't that a
reference to Iran and aren't the Iranians Persians, not
Arabs? What is the relationship between Moslem states and
Arabs? I ought to do my homework, but I want to put this
down before I do, for it is representative, I believe, of
our ignorance of a vital area of the world and the
heritage of a significant if (I think) relatively small
American population. I am not proud of my ignorance, but
I think it useful once in a while (a very long while) to
admit to the class that we, too, have gaps in our
knowledge. (Meanwhile, I still want to quarrel a little
with the article. There was, after all, Lawrence of
Arabia!)
   Shaheen is surely right, however, that "America's
bogeyman is the Arab," perhaps even more so now that the
Evil Empire seems to have moved into a glass-nost house
and is not so busy, as we officially believed, throwing
stones. The image of Arabs is thus the best place to
attack stereotyping. We are sure to get blistered for
using Jewish stereotypes or black or Native American, but
because there is a media-consensus and perhaps a majority
consensus that Arabs are bad guys, dirty terrorists, our
stereotypes of Arabs are less likely to be challenged,
making them I think all the more worth challenging.
   I've tried a couple of ways of going about this: the
disinterested, asking the class to write a description of
an Arab or the "typical" Arab, or, asking them to
describe the stereotype of the Arab. I have had very few
Arabs or Arab-Americans in class, so I have not been able
to get "inside views." The few times I have asked

students to write out the Arab stereotype and then check it against Arabs they have known have not worked very well. It may be worth going through the motions, however, to suggest that it is precisely because we do not know very many Arab(-Americans) that the stereotype is so unchallenged.


James Fallows
THE JAPANESE ARE DIFFERENT FROM YOU AND ME

Nonfiction; European-American in Japan
    Because there are few reasonably lengthy expository essays in this volume, I try to make use of this one, when appropriate to the course, to explore some of the structures and strategies of expository prose. (Now that I have a volume with a short piece like Shaheen's immediately preceding Fallows, I might get some things up front earlier.) I'll just indicate some points that I treat at somewhat greater length in class.
    I first take the extraordinary step of beginning at the beginning--with the first sentence. I hope your students regularly write more grabbing--or at least fetching--opening sentences than mine do. I don't get much of "In this modern day and age of ours of today . . . " openings anymore, but I do get a whole spectrum of dull ones. "Japan is turning me into Mrs. Trollope" gives us something to shoot for. Even for those (all) who have never heard of Mr. Trollope (the son) much less Mrs. Trollope, the sentence works (maybe beyond Fallows' conscious intent): turning him into a trollope, turning him into a Mrs. For those who know Mrs. Trollope, especially those from Cincinnati, who, as I remember, she did not treat very well, the opening has a similar impact, though for different reasons. For our students, the second sentence explains the intended sense of the first, like the definition of a foreign word.
    I like distinctions. Of course I like connections but I don't like to "only connect"; so Fallows' early distinction between "different" and "wrong" sets me off. When the distinctions also involve cultural differences, as Fallows does when he cites some of the differences between Japanese and Western culture, they play to another one of my prejudices: the moral and aesthetic value of seeing things from a different, unusual perspective. Who could imagine that butter would be offensive--bland, innocent <u>butter</u> of all things?
    I then turn to structure--and sometimes ask the class to outline the essay. Besides the divisions into different and better, there is the strategy of setting up the American reader to feel somewhat uncomfortable (unless masochistic) by focusing on superior automobile production, mechanical and human competence, dedication

to quality work and service, and the relative classlessness. Some words here and there prepare for the shift, like "almost tribal society" in par. 5, but probably par. 9 marks the transition; and it is a paragraph about transition, the transition from "honored guest" to "resident alien," a move from good to not so good.

Then comes the first zinger--a surprise to those who do not know Japan, and never a part of our stereotype of the Japanese--pornography. Like the opening sentence, this opening of the case for the prosecution has dramatic impact. Though the prevalence of pornography in Japan may be shocking, the second charge, racism, is, if less dramatic, more serious. Fallows clearly knows what he is about, building masterfully to another switch (Japanese racism in its view of the West is both a claim of superiority and a fear of inferiority), and to an indictment of their closed, insular, parochial society. He suggests ours is open and, no matter how imperfectly practiced, an inclusive one.

Fallows's case is a good one, but I have to watch out, since most of my classes are predominatly Caucasian, that the net result is not a feeling of superiority or even a hostility toward the Japanese. I like to remind the class, finally, that the essay is about Japanese culture and society, <u>not</u> a definition of what a Japanese man or woman is like or is worth. In this regard, I find the title slightly misleading and a little dangerous in its ambiguity. Ironically, from the title and the criticism of Japanese culture, the essay can be construed as racist, the last thing that Fallows would want.


Mark Salzman
TEACHER WEI

Nonfiction; European-American in China
Just in case your class, or certain members of it, thought you, or me or the text, racist and anti-Oriental (or themselves were inclined to jump to ugly conclusions), this charming autobiographical piece ought to dispel the miasma. I find this just as much a study of contrasts, of differences and better/worse as the Fallows piece. Some of my students think Salzman comes through as immodest; unlike the usual Oscar or Emmy or MVP winner, he doesn't say "I don't deserve this. I owe it to my coach (drama, volleyball, acting) and all the little people who helped me (my team) be a winner." I confess I felt a little bit of brashness and even self-satisfaction coming through, especially, perhaps, in his lecture on *E.T.* But upon reflection, I've come to believe that this is a brilliantly subtle way of dramatizing whole concepts and cultures: his "overacting," his "larger than

life" presentation, his exuberance and extroversion and overstatement are all "American" in the sense that John Bunyan and tall tales and political oratory and hype are "American." And this is contrasted here with the subtle, indirect and understated character that shows up throughout the piece in the Chinese people, especially but not only, in Teacher Wei. And there is as well a refreshing outgoingness for all the subtlety and indirection, humanity and warmth in relationships, an unselfishness that contrasts with our sex-and-success public life. This contrast even surprises Salzman, the student of things Chinese who by his academic and other choices has tried to realize different kinds of relationships.

I find this teaches well with Fallows. Not only do we get a positive side to match Fallows' rather negative portrait of Asian cultures, but I can also reinforce some of the observations I made or elicited about structure and strategy in the Fallows essay. The first paragraph, for example, perhaps even the first sentence, has the attention-grabbing quality we noted in Fallows. And if Fallows is, in the early stages of the essay, rather positive about the Japanese only to qualify and undercut that impression later, Salzman puts the worst Chinese foot (the "most worst," the bound feet of the women being a thing of the past now, officially) forward. And yet, by the end of the paragraph the "bad impression"--the attendant closing the doors on a man hanging half out of the bus--dissolves as the man cheerfully pays his fare at the end of the paragraph. What we are left with, instead of a negative or positive response, my students affirm, is a puzzlement, a mystery, a real sense of difference. (And you know how I love perspectival and behavioral differences.) Salzman suggests a more mundane, material difference in the second paragraph, when, having bought a bike and paid for it in cash, he feels "as if I had walked into a car dealer, paid for a Porsche in cash, and driven it out of the showroom right through the floor-to-ceiling windows."

After I ask the class to look at the first two paragraphs, and, sometimes, after I suggest they outline the selection, I have them list all the unexpected or strange events described in the story, beginning with the man who cheerfully pays his fare after having had the bus door slammed shut on him halfway onto the vehicle. Then, if we have time, I ask for the rationale they deduce from the behavior and thought of the Chinese characters that seems to be behind their actions--like Teacher Wei's bringing rice liquor to the lessons. Not only do I not usually bring liquor to conferences, I cannot call to mind behavior in others that is analogous to that of Teacher Wei and Dr. Li here. Nevertheless, sometimes my students come up with an example or two. It's worth asking about, I find. (Much of the time the incidents told me are somewhat like the advice Teacher Wei gives Salzman not to laugh at his own jokes too much, too much laughter causing digestive problems. The world seems full of Chinese-Jewish mothers of all ethnic kinds.)

## Countee Cullen
## INCIDENT

Poem; Afro-American
  As the study question suggests, I feel the nature of the incident and the verse form clash, the ugly and the jaunty jarring together. That does not mean I think the poem therefore bad. As a matter of fact I believe that contradiction, almost the equivalent of cacophony, gives the poem a kind of macabre power. Too, the naive language--"Heart-filled, head-filled with glee" ("glee" is a "literary" word, perhaps, but chiefly in the works of amateurs)--lends a certain pathos: poor, innocent kid, to run into such a disturbing incident. Not all my students agree with me; some find the poem, not the speaker, naive and awkward. I try to read aloud a few Scots ballads, but it doesn't always do any good. As long as they and I both agree as to what's <u>there</u>, I don't mind our not judging or feeling the same about what's there.

## Sharon Olds
## ON THE SUBWAY

Poem; White-black
  I like to teach this poem along with the Countee Cullen one that precedes it here. Is there any chance, I sometimes ask, that the eight year-old in the Cullen poem could have grown into this boy on the subway? How old do you imagine the boy is? On what evidence? Gender aside, is there any chance that the young Baltimorean could have grown up to be the speaker of the Olds poem? I am hoping to get into a discussion of context, of what has happened in race relations in the past half-century that makes the Olds poem seem distinctly modern or recent. But then I turn the tables a bit: Can you imagine The Incident happening <u>now</u>? in Baltimore? New York? Peoria? What does that suggest has or has not happened in the past few generations? And how about the comforting assumption that if we just let the children alone all racial problems would readily resolve themselves? Is eight years old too old?

But I do not want to talk about this poem only in
terms of the general racial issue. I sometimes do not
assign the poem but have it read in class. On such
occasions I stress "expectation" (the literary element
discussed at the end of this chapter). I have a student
begin the poem and then stop him or her at the period in
line 9 and ask either the reader or the class in general
what their expectations are, what they think is going to
happen. Then, another reader, and at the middle of l.21,
STOP! First we talk about the images: "red, like the
inside of the body," "the / whole skin of an animal," "his
raw face," and then "his power," "my power," and the
speaker "eating the steak he does not eat." What do we
expect now?

Then, perhaps, we return to the racial issue. Of what
races are the speaker and the boy? How do we know (if
we've read only to the middle of l. 21)? It's only later
in that line that he is identified as black. But we knew
all along, didn't we, I ask the class. How? What does it
mean that we knew?

And then we get to the last lines of the poem and
the insistence that all of white society profits from the
subjugation of blacks, so that all whites--not just those
slaveholders of old--are guilty of benefiting from
racism. Do your students believe that? If so, what are
they prepared to do about it?

Circling back once more to imagery, what do your
students get from the last five lines or so of the poem?
I like to let them say, because then they cannot repeat
that old canard that all English teachers want to talk
about is sex.


                    Leslie Marmon Silko
                     [LONG TIME AGO]

Poem; Native American (Laguna) and Chicana
        To answer my last study question, I cannot make much
out of the shape. Is it a totem pole? Is there a mushroom
cloud rising up from l. 176 to l. 148 or so? What do your
students think? I cannot promise prizes, but I would like
to hear.
        It is the dark peoples' witch that calls up the
white terror, the greatest horror of the many horrors at
the meeting. (The witch, by the way, is not identified by
nationality or sex [ll.66-69] which somehow makes it more
ominous and "Martian.") The chief charge against the
whites who will come is the familiar one of their divorce
from nature, their treatment of life-forms as objects
(ll. 90-100). You might ask students to look back over
earlier Native American pieces to see if this charge and
its counterpart (that Native Americans are somehow close
to and in tune with nature) is a common theme, and you

might alert them to look for that theme later. My students have a hard time with this, and it soon gets to be a discussion of "development" versus "conservation": should we not build houses out of wood? or maufacture paper from pulp? or make shoes and even motorcycle jackets from hide? Do we really want to go back to nature and give up VCRs and videos? And how destructive have we actually been? Aren't there about as many Native Americans now as there were when Columbus landed? And if it is true that "we" brought tuberculosis and venereal diseases, did we not also raise the life expectancy of "native peoples" all over the world? If you're not careful your students, like mine, will get on to saving the whales, the ozone layer, acid rain, and the like. Whether you give them their head depends on how much time and patience you have.

I try not to let it go on too long, for I do want to get to "the power of narrative" and the imagination. When the witch promises or threatens a story, the other witches laugh, but it says that as the story is told it will begin to happen (ll. 80-81). And at the end, the other witches ask that the story be called back, but it cannot be. Of course we know that the "prophecy" did come true, but was the story the product of some form of second sight or did it actually create the disaster that was to come? Is the imagination, story-telling, a self-fulfilling prophecy? And if the poem says this, does such a belief come out of the "primitive" imagination of those who lived a long time ago, or is it a very sophisticated concept of narratology or of ontology?


Maxine Hong Kingston
THE WILD MAN OF THE GREEN SWAMP

Narrative; Chinese-American
The headnote recommends that students read the title and first paragraph and write down their expectations. You may want to ask a few to read their "predictions." Did any of them notice the clause, "he made strange noises as in a foreign language and ran back into the saw grass"? Mine do not, usually. How sneaky of Kingston, for of course he is speaking a foreign language, but the "as" becomes "as if" for most of us, a simile and therefore not "literal." The paragraph ends with the conjecture about the wild man being a bear, but, characteristically, Kingston does not let that red herring smell long--the second paragraph begins by telling us a game officer saw a man. Kingston is not focusing on "suspense" in the usual way, only in little short bursts. There is mystery, for "no one could live in the swamp" (par. 3), but by the fifth paragraph the mystery is over. I like to work this first part of the piece for all it's worth, sometimes

comparing it to the opening of the Fallows and Salzman pieces as ways of engaging the reader immediately. Here I sometimes ask the students to imagine (and occasionally to write down) a version of the narrative beginning something like this:

> In 1975 a Chinese man who had jumped ship was found to have lived in Green Swamp, Florida, a mosquito-infested marsh inhabited by man-eating animals, a place where no one was thought to be able to live.

I use this version to talk about structure and how the "same" story can be a quite different story depending on how it is told. A simple proposition, but one students are not always aware of; they think certain facts and selection and order of telling are all "given" or fixed, somehow. This can be a useful exercise both for a writing exercise and a "reading lesson."

The story of the misunderstanding that plagued the "Wild Man" because of his foreignness and the hardships he underwent as a result are certainly an indictment of the suspicion of and ignorance about "aliens." Yet I don't think many who read the first eight and a half paragraphs of the piece expect the ninth paragraph to end as it does, with the man's suicide—a measure of the man's desperation. You might ask students to explain the shift in par. 10 back to the time he was taken from the swamp, and you might want to ask whether this shift seems a narrative strategy or a polemical one, a way of driving a point home.

The shift in the final paragraph, marked by the break on the page, makes the same point but, it seems to me, with quite a different effect. The new, black Wild Man universalizes the "alien" or "Martian" theme, it is true, but what is the force of his wearing a shirt but no pants? Are the newspapers right, this time? Is this Wild Man crazy? The ambivalence here is, I believe, functional: we need to know a great deal more about the aliens before we judge them or their sanity. Perhaps the ending is clearer than that and the ambivalence is only my lack of understanding, but it is useful in any case, to open up the possibility that sometimes there is no thematic closure. (The last clause of the story adds another twist. Is it the police who are "crazy"? Do the police represent the official view of the state, and "we" the popular view, that of ordinary people? Wild, man.)

Katherine Anne Porter
HOLIDAY

Short story; Regional/German-American

This is one of the few pieces in the volume by a
"canonical" figure. Our internal guideline was that if we
ran across a splendid cross-cultural piece by a canonical
figure, we would include it only if it were a
noncanonical, seldom-if-ever-antholgized work. "Holiday"
fits that description. It is also useful in that the
"other" is a rather familiar ethnic group that, because
of its numbers, Northern European origin, and general
WASPishness, is seldom thought of as "other," and even
less often as "exotically other" or very different.
Finally, the noncultural alienating factor of retardation
in this tale makes its "Martian" theme more complex.

Despite my valiant effort to make students feel that
this story has us asking, what's going to happen next? or
at least, what is going to happen?--the obvious intention
of the first study question--there are always some
students who will find "Holiday" slow-moving,
particularly at first. (One could make a case that
Porter's first two paragraphs, in which she talks about
the story as a story, is an attempt to stimulate
expectation somewhat artificly, giving her a chance to
dwell in a somewhat leisurely fashion on details in the
early portions of the story.) That's also why I ask about
the "irrelevant details" in pars. 16 & 17: they are
simultaneously relevant and irrelevant, I believe. That
is, though the narrator says "I studied the harness, a
real mystery," it is not that much of a mystery for the
reader who does not really care why the harness "met and
clung in all sorts of unexpected places." It does not
impel the reader breathlessly forward or make the reader
concentrate on the details trying to fathom their import.
Yet, by hindsight, the harness is an emblem of the life
on the farm as she will discover it, full of the
unexpected, the risky, the surprisingly important
"seemingly unimportant" details. Porter works both to
keep us interested--expectant and curious--and to slow
down our reading so that we dwell on the details,
including the details of the language (thus my fourth
study question about the similes).

Slowing down, dwelling on the language is worth it.
Porter's language to me is gorgeous, rich in
psychological and cosmic analysis, as in paragraphs 27
and 83, laden with passages fusing the descriptive and
"spiritual," like par. 58, and full of just plain
wonderful sentences, like this from par. 82, after the
narrator has touched Ottilie's skin: "My sense of her
realness, her humanity, this shattered being that was a
woman, was so shocking to me that a howl as doglike and
despairing as her own rose in me unuttered and died

again, to be a perpetual ghost" (oh, that last phrase!).
I have to watch out, because I can easily slow my class
down by reading out or having them read out passage after
glorious passage.

There are a lot of thematic handles you can grab
here besides the Martian one. Though the story may not
create a great sense of suspenseful expectation, it is in
some ways about expectations, asking us what we expect
out of life. The family's stoic acceptance of their lot,
the dedication to their work and their familial-communal
life, even the way they ignore, exploit, but make a place
for Ottilie, all these things  educate the narrator, show
her that she too is a "fool of life," has work to do in
the world, and should do so without complaint. But this
is not masochistic or Puritanic self-denial for the sake
of self-denial--there are troubles you are a fool not to
run from as well as those which are truly yours and which
you must accept, as the narrator in the first paragraph
says she is later to learn.

I also pay attention to the center of self
articulated in par. 27, the connection of that center
with the center of Ottilie (par. 58), and the core of
sorrow in each of us that unites in communal grief
(par. 77). In contrast, the recognition that there is a
limit to what we can do for another, that reality remains
intransigent (par. 83) provides another complicated
thematic web.

I have not even mentioned the whole concept of
holiday, of an apparent time out from our sequential-
consequential everyday life. But you will no doubt have
your own handles to grab in this rich and complex story.


Carter Revard
DISCOVERY OF THE NEW WORLD

Poem; Extra-terrestrial, with allusion to European
"discovery" of native America

I like to use my "stop-and-go" projection technique
here, asking students to read a sentence at a time, but
with a slight difference. Usually I ask them to note
carefully what they expect to happen next. That can be
done here too, but I try slyly to suggest that they
record their expectations "and anything else interesting
they notice or are thinking about." The reason is that
this poem can occasion a more complex description of the
reading process.

The formal element discussed in the afterword to
this chapter is "expectation" and there is a certain
amount of conjecture here about what will happen next.
But I find this incisive poem useful to talk about all
three dimensions of reading--processing the text,
projecting or anticipating what will come next,

recapitulation or recovery of what has gone before--and I
like to emphasize here the retroactive or recovery
dimension. It is conceivable that a few readers will
catch the "New World" clue in the title and so will read
the whole poem as a metaphor or analogue of the European
"discovery" of America. But most will not catch on for
some time (is the Sherman reference, though accurate, a
red herring, leading us away from Columbus and all
that?), many not until very near the end, and a few not
until it is pointed out to them. Each of these readers
will have a diferent first-reading experience of the
poem. All will have a perspective similar to that of
those readers who "knew from the beginning." What happens
to the first-time readers who do not catch the parallel
until about the middle of the poem or thereafter? How
much detail do you or can you hold in your mind, most of
it backgrounded, when you do not have some center or
interpretation or point to hang your memory of the detail
on? Isn't there a special thrill in recognizing the
parallel in a particularly clever detail--"we'll get to
study / the way our heart attacks and cancers spread among
them, / since they seem not immune to these" (substituting
for tuberculosis, pneumonia, venereal disease,
alcoholism, and all the other benefits of western
civilization visited upon the natives)?
     A supplementary exercise might be--once everyone is
in on the gag--to have students go back through the poem
"interpreting" all the space-man details. There are bound
to be--if your experience is like mine--rather wild
conjectures, similarities seen that few others in the
class will agree with. Depending upon the course in which
this text is being used and the nature and context of the
class, you might want to draw the parallel with the
typological reading of the details of the Old Testament
as prophetic of the New--Samson as Christ, etc.--and the
illuminating power and dangers of analogy.
     I don't know whether we are truly more humane
nowadays or just more hypocritical and self-deceiving,
but I find few students who do not claim to see the
justice of the Native American cause and the culpability
of the explorers and settlers.


                    Margaret Atwood
                    THE MAN FROM MARS

Short story; Vietnamese in Canada
     As you will have noticed in the first study
question, I continue here briefly the "recovery"
dimension of the reading process dwelled on in discussing
the Carter Revard poem. "A long time ago . . ." is both
indicative and misleading: it refers to the period not
long before the Vietnam war.

The story is useful, coming as it does at the end of a chapter, to look back not only over this particular chapter but to focus on one of the main themes of the book, cross-cultural experience (and its ugly underside, racism). Here I like to begin with the periphery, with Christine's mother, and her attitudes, explicit and implicit, toward "persons from another culture" as she would put it, calling attention to the limits of "another": that is, French is okay for WASP Christine (after all, she's having trouble getting a man of her own culture) but truly other, racially other, that is another matter. I don't expect too much difficulty in ferreting this out of the class. Where I do expect a certain amount of difficulty is in the more subtle "affirmative" racism of Christine herself. Thus study question 4, "Why does Christine give the stranger her name?" is meant to point to a passage in which Christine's leaning over backwards because the stranger is of a different race is meant to put the students on that track, as is the study question (10) about her relationship to Elvira. And I like to point out that the "affirmative" side does hide racism that is not always and in all ways affirmative; thus study question 5 about Christine's fear and its pointing to par. 28.

In this text and context it is inevitable that we concentrate on the crosscultural dimension of this story, but I try not to limit the discussion to that. It is not often that the "romantic" heroine of a story is big and overweight--"statuesque," her mother says, but this is, I believe, a moving, pathetic, and original (and sometimes funny) aspect of Atwood's story. We often pooh-pooh romances with the perfectly beautiful heroine but we are also sometimes uncomfortable when the heroine is not highly attractive (we forget, perhaps do not even believe, Jane Eyre is as mousy as she says--modesty, no doubt). The let-down when the "Martian" is arrested in Montreal for molesting a sixty year-old Mother Superior is painful (par. 159). Asking students to trace the physical description of Christine, her self-image, and the height or depth of her self-esteem might make an interesting exercise (I haven't tried it yet--let me know, if you do, how it comes out). The theme of physical appearance as a (flawed) barometer of personal worth is not that far from the issue of racism, and the two can be related profitably in the discussion of this story, I believe. And the whole story is framed, from the first four words to the last three paragraphs, by the war, and question 6 points to the irony of Christine's side winning the debate in which it argued that war is obsolete. The inhumanity of war, and the relative triviality of racial difference in the face of the

universal human catastrophe of war, reveals another
intricate interrelationship in this tightly woven though
seemingly casually or informally constructed story.

Conflict comes up more frequently and insistently in this chapter than in any other section of the book. The whole idea of constructing barriers between people, for whatever reason, leads repeatedly to confrontation.  At the end of the chapter, we have provided a short essay relating conflict to structure, and you might wish to read it quickly before you begin teaching any of the selections, just to remind yourself of traditional ways of describing how conflict serves as the basis for the structure and movement of plays.  Probably you will not want to do much with structure per se early on in the chapter, but you may wish to look to some of the issues by getting your students to watch regularly for how conflict is introduced, how its intensification and complication build action and tension, how it is resolved, and what remains to be done in words after the central crisis takes place.  All this can be done with a minimum of technical terminology--or with no technical terms at all--and it can be useful for students to discuss issues of structure first in stories, which they usually find more familiar and congenial, before they are faced with trying to "see" (almost literally) the structure of a play on stage.  The first story here, because it contains several different confrontation scenes stretched across a given backdrop of conflict from the very beginning, offers a good first shot at questions of structure.  Usually I do not--at least in asking students to describe for themselves how a plot is built and presented--use either the term <u>structure</u> or the term <u>form</u>.  Rather I begin by asking them to describe in what <u>order</u> facts are presented, how the author has <u>organized</u> a story, what kinds of <u>sequences</u> are involved, what information is held back.  <u>Form</u> and <u>structure</u> remain pretty abstract terms to most students, and useful as they ultimately are for understanding the emotional impact upon the audience and for showing how something that has been created must be resolved and dissipated before closure can occur, the terms are confusing if introduced too early. I find it especially important ultimately to distinguish between form and structure, between the outward appearance and the internal principles of cohesion and strength. I have pretty good luck making the distinction by referring to buildings under construction, but forcing distinctions early creates resistance, and often it is better to have some issues of organization and presentation out on the table before labels are firmly attached.

Ralph Ellison
BATTLE ROYAL

Short story; Afro-American
     It is worth spending time on setting and detail here
before getting at the tensions and conflicts.  Beyond
getting students to mention in class the various details
and what each detail individually contributes, it is
important to ask them why so much detail accumulates and
how detail, especially as language gives it value and
emotional coloring, sets up the reader for feelings and
attitudes. I also like to spend time on the way the
narrator presents himself because such a discussion leads
to a second form of conflict that is easy to pass over
with the racial conflict so blatant and so compelling.
     That second conflict involves the different worlds
of adolescents and adults and the anxieties of growing
up. Often it is useful to introduce other initiation
stories (stories about growing up) into the discussion
here, either stories you have taught earlier in the
course or new ones you can introduce here for comparison.
(Stories earlier in the book that work well include
Anthony's "Sandra Street," Gilchrist's "Traveler," and
Kadohata's "Charlie-O"; the "classic" stories that many
English teachers like to use to illustrate the standard
initiation theme in modern life are Hemingway's stories.)
     Once you have gotten the students to see how much
this story is like standard initiation stories, though,
it is important to go back to the racial theme and show
how the narrator's growing up here has an added
dimension:  he has to understand how to continue to
appear naive and child-like so that the white adults do
not think him too smart, uppity, rebellious, or
potentially successful.  You are a very good teacher if
you are able to restrain the discussion here to issues of
self-consciousness rather than letting it become a
discussion, leaving the story altogether behind, of the
expectations of behavior across various cultural lines.
But of course you may wish to let such a discussion
develop for a while. It can certainly be healthy
culturally--and even useful literarily and critically--to
get some of these highly charged issues out into the
open, especially if you are teaching a class in writing
and want to draw on this discussion for student writing
assignments.  "Battle Royal," incidentally, works
extremely well as a model for students writing about
their own experiences in growing up.

Leo Romero
WHAT THE GOSSIPS SAW

Poem; Chicano
Fences <u>within</u> groups are important to this poem, and
this selection is especially useful for making the point,
early in this chapter, that fences are of many different
kinds, erected by different people for very different
reasons. Get them to discuss where their sympathies lie
here and show you exactly how--and where in the poem--
those sympathies are engaged.


R. T. Smith
RED ANGER

Poem; Native American
A good discussion of rhetorical strategies can
result from questions about why three different tribes
are described briefly rather than giving exclusive--and
more intensive--attention to one tribe or even one single
detail.


Donna Kate Rushin
THE BRIDGE POEM

Poem; Afro-American
Here the victim of "fences" is the person caught
between forces, rather than someone who is fenced out or
in, and it is interesting to talk about how sympathy is
generated for her plight. Discuss where the anger is
directed and how. Get students to talk about the
strength of emotion early in the poem and how it is
expressed. This poem is a good model for student
writing: its deceptively simple organization makes
students feel that they can talk, almost directly, in
verse about private feelings. If you use it as a writing
model, get the students to talk fully about the poem
<u>first</u>, going into evaluative detail in class about what
aspects of self-expression work best and which work least
well. Ask them to evaluate the conversational repetition,
to defend its aims; ask them to provide a rationale for
the directness too, and don't let them get away with
cheap shots about its "stream of consciousness," lack of
organization, or uncalculated self-indulgence.

Pat Mora
SONRISAS

Poem; Chicana
    This is a good poem to teach on the same day as the
Rushin poem above.  In effect, it places the speaker in a
similar position but uses very different strategies to
make its point.  After you discuss each poem separately--
emphasizing the crisp, concise, clean images and the
binary quality that dramatize the speaker's plight here--
get your students to compare the two methods and list the
advantages of each strategy.  Try to keep them from using
either poem to abuse the other one, getting them to see
instead that wholly different models of organization and
rhetoric are involved.  The Mora poem works so well for
formalist analysis that there are advantages in teaching
this poem earlier in the hour: it is easier to make the
transition to the more emotional and less formal than the
other way round.  You will probably find that your
students are quite good in class at explaining how the
Mora poem works because its contrasts are so clear and
clean and directly set up.  They may have more trouble
expressing themselves about the virtues of Rushin, even
though the method there is more likely to resemble their
own processes of formulation and expression.


Edward Corsi
I BEHOLD AMERICA

Nonfiction; Italian-American
    This is a good selection in which to return to
issues of memory.  Specifically, look at the effect of
two different time frames upon the narrative focus,
especially if you first took up this issue very early in
the course when your students' sensibilities and skills
were relatively undeveloped.  It is also worth spending
class time here on the subdued tenor of the tone.  A lot
of powerful material is presented, and feelings obviously
run deep, but the emotions often seem suppressed.  Get
your students to evaluate the strategies of restraint,
perhaps drawing on the discussion of the Mora and Rushin
poems above.  I like to cross-reference discussions in
this way so that students get the idea that, whatever
crucial differences there are among species and genres,
language often produces similar effects across generic
and modal boundaries; the "subtext" here is that writers,
including the students themselves once they gain a little
experience and develop some self-consciousness and
calculation, make specific decisions about what to
include and what not to include, what stance to take,
what tone to employ even _after_ they have made a basic
decision about aim and form.

James Seilsopour
I FORGOT THE WORDS TO THE NATIONAL ANTHEM

Nonfiction; Iranian-American
    I find that this unpretentious essay is strangely
moving to students--even when feelings against Iran were
at their most feverish height.  Maybe the fact that
Seilsopour wrote this essay when he was younger than our
students are now is responsible; more likely it has to do
with the fact that almost all students have experienced
(or feared) the kind of isolation, for whatever reason,
from their peers that Seilsopour describes so vividly
here.  Still, students don't often talk about the piece
well in class, perhaps because it seems relatively
uncalculated, but more likely because the political and
psychological issues here become so entangled as to
inhibit public discussion.  Students often brood over the
piece later.  A writing exercise, using this essay as a
model, can be very useful.  I like to insist that they
make up an incident to write a personal account of: that
tends to raise their deepest anxieties to articulation
instead of letting them off the hook by describing a
personal, and thus more threatening, episode.


Michelle Cliff
IF I COULD WRITE THIS IN FIRE I WOULD WRITE THIS IN FIRE

Nonfiction; Jamaican-American
    This is about as close to written in fire, or some
other pure, beyond-verbal substance, as you can get. The
power it generates in the classroom is overwhelming.  The
classroom difficulty is certainly not getting students
interested responding to its points or seeing relevance
or implications.  The difficulty is in getting them to
talk about it rationally and in terms of the sources of
its rhetorical effectiveness.  The immediacy of emotion,
freshness, sincerity, etc. are easy enough to respond to,
but students are apt to think that powerful effect comes
from powerful feeling, period.  Get them to compare other
selections which are more restrained, in which anger
seeps or bursts through, with the directness here. Get
them to see the calculation in this essay--how pieces of
the long-ago past are interwoven with more recent events
and bursts of emotion.  I get them to outline it,
pointing out the transitions and the places where
transitions are notably, calculatedly omitted.  I get
them to list all the self-conscious gestures of
spontaneity and immediacy ("An interesting face...," " A
true story . . .," "There is no ending to this piece of
writing.") I ask them to list all the themes and topics
covered in these pages and explain how they become
interrelated.  The classroom task here is to get students

to see what a complex, <u>finished</u> piece of writing it is
when everything, from the title on, presents itself as if
it were offhand, just an outburst of feeling.  Starting
with the title--a good idea with a lot of selec-
tions--is particularly useful here to suggest the kind of
rhetorical stance the author assumes from the start.

But don't let your students get <u>too</u> far away from
the naked emotional power of the anger here.  Get them to
analyze the sources of anger, not just its rhetoric.
Different students will have different favorite parts,
based largely (in my experience) upon which sections of
the essay are closest to their own experience.  Let them
talk about their favorite anecdotes, phrases, or devices.
Because intention and effect are so closely in tune here,
this selection is especially good for getting students to
see how language is power.  I like to use this selection
as the model for a writing assignment, inviting students
to be a bit more freewheeling than usual, but I insist
they begin from some real or imagined autobiographical
anecdote and restrict them to a short format.  And I
insist that they analyze their own prose and evaluate the
effects they are able to produce through unorthodox
organizational strategies.


nila northSun
UP AND OUT

Poem; Native American (Shoshone-Chippewa)
A good poem to use for comparison is Maurice Kenny's
"Going Home."  Here the emphasis is less on material
well-being than on basic values, and it is worth having
your students list the different <u>things</u> (and what they
represent) in Reservation and post-Reservation life.
What kind of conclusion does northSun draw about the
values Native Americans take with them when they leave
the Reservation?  Where do those values come from?  Who
seems to be in charge of values?  How free do individuals
seem to be to choose alternative values?  What forces
restrict their freedom?


Dwight Okita
IN RESPONSE TO EXECUTIVE ORDER 9066: ALL AMERICANS OF
JAPANESE DESCENT MUST REPORT TO RELOCATION CENTERS

Poem; Japanese-American
The tone of this poem is so deftly managed that its
effects are quite spectacular. It is a good idea to get
the class to try to account for the poem's ability to do
so much emotionally in so little space.  Ask about the
humor in the friendship with Denise.  How do they know
the speaker is <u>not</u> a copier on tests?  What does the joke

about baldness tell us about the speaker?  Why does the
poem pretend to be addressed to the impersonal
government?  What is accomplished by the self-deprecating
details about a messy room and bad spelling? What is
accomplished by the indication of what the speaker
intends to take with her to the relocation center?


August Wilson
FENCES

Play; Afro-American
    I suggest three different approaches to this play:
one emphasizing the theme of this chapter, one involving
characterization (the characters here are not only
clearly and firmly drawn, but the playwright takes bold
chances with type characters that he goes on to
individuate carefully), and one having to do with the
play's staging and dramatic structure.
    The discussion of theme can grow most naturally out
of the fence on stage. In its unfinished state in plain
sight through most of the play, the fence is a visual
reminder of intentional barriers (as well as of
incompleteness and lack of control).  The fence here,
even in Troy's intentions, stands for something different
from a lot of the fences in the selections earlier in the
chapter. In defining exactly what it represents to Troy,
to Rose, and to us as audience, you can run back over the
possible symbolisms suggested by what fences stand for--
or stand between--in other pieces of writing.  The study
questions will set up this discussion quite fully for the
class. Indeed, you may well have set up the discussion
more fully than you expect if you have varied, in your
teaching of other selections, your emphasis on the idea
of how barriers work and how different kinds of people
use barriers for their own psychological reasons. (You
will no doubt wish to discuss in some detail the fences
between generations, genders, and friends, too; in fact,
a good strategy to begin the discussion is to get your
students to list all the kinds of fences they can think
of that appear literally or metaphorically in the play.)
    My favorite character to use to show how subtly the
play develops its characterization is Gabriel.  In a way
he is purely a stage "type"--the "crazy" who is not all
there but is sweet as pie and in his innocence represents
a kind of norm.  And, of course, Gabriel performs that
role admirably, his simplicity offering at several
crucial places a welcome relief from the human
complexities that "regular" characters can't cope with.
But let your students show each other how much more
complex Gabriel turns out to be.  Get them to point out
where he becomes a complication, even a pain in the neck
to the audience as well as to the Maxons.  Several other

characters also work off "type" models but are well individuated. If you have taught other plays earlier in the course, you might wish to use whatever character you choose to isolate here as a vehicle to note how, in different plays, different authors individualize figures who begin with some burden of type but become complicated by their function in the play.

The afterword to the chapter will serve as a reminder to your students about the traditional terms used to describe dramatic structure, and once you have the play's themes and ideas on the table, you may want to have the students point specifically to divisions in the play that correspond to classic structural divisions. One thing that may confuse them at first--and it is deliberate on our part--is that structure is put in terms of a five-act play, whereas Wilson has divided his play into only two acts, presented in the way most contemporary plays are with a single intermission. Get them to reconcile the two conventions; let them know that act division is only a convention while structural matters transcend such obvious formal markings. Different students will want to mark the points slightly differently, of course. It is always a risk to have this sort of class discussion because there is usually no single "right" answer in a seamless play. But you can show yourself to be at once sensible and flexible by being tolerant of different possible locations and getting students to support different positions instead of refereeing them into a quick corner. The point is to get them to see that the action does in fact rise, come to a crisis, then fall to a point where a resolution and closure can occur.

Some discussion of visualness seems necessary for this play, and for me the most convenient way of leading into it is to return to the issue of the fence. The question, which you can pose just as profitably at the end as at the beginning, is how to stage the fence, using it as a silent commentary on the action taking place all around it but without making explicit reference to it. If you have begun with a thematic discussion of fences and ended with dramatic structure, you can do a kind of afterpiece on staging that picks up those two threads.

## O. Henry
## THE COMING-OUT OF MAGGIE

Short story; Irish-American and Italian-American
We are likely to have more problems with this story
than are our students, for the form of humor and irony
here is somewhat like that of the school (including high
school) newspaper. It seems so blatant it is difficult
for us to think of the story as "literature." Perhaps
recent critical theories and trends downplaying the
Jamesian and even the Joycean, the "disappearance of the
author" and the illusion of realism, will let us look
again at works of this type. I'm not entirely ready, but
I do find the story a useful one for talking about
overstatement and understatement and irony--and I do find
it a bit more subtle and a lot more ambivalent than I
used to. Here's the kind of thing I do/say/try to bring
out:
We usually associate verbal <u>irony</u> with reticence or
"understatement," where the words mean more than they
seem to say ("Go ahead, make my day."). O. Henry's irony,
however, comes from "overstatement," where the language
is fancier or more high-flown than the subject matter
seems to deserve, somewhat like the mock heroic. The O.
Henry irony is also rather self-conscious, heavy-handed,
and obvious. See, for example, par. 4, which is clearly a
highfalutin way of saying that Maggie, having a date
for the first time, is having a good time. The tone of
the story as a whole, however, is not so simple or
obvious; it is not entirely clear whether O. Henry's
ironic humor is good-natured or bitter.
This doubt or ambivalence pervades the entire story,
so that we are frequently not too sure what attitude we
are meant to take towards the characters and their
actions. We are led to sympathize with poor Maggie
throughout the story, for example, but at the end we may
feel we must separate ourselves from her and her
attitudes; we may not be too sure whether we want her to
win or lose, and not too sure what the story is "saying."
The ambivalence or irony is evident at the end in the
title: Maggie comes out but does not come out.
I don't often find myself able to get this into the
discussion, but the form of the story is also ambivalent.
Classical comedy often treats the destabilization of a
society by the appearance of an outsider and the return
to harmony though the ejection of that outsider. It is
not certain that the ejection of "Terry" is comic in
either the popular or literary sense, though the

elaborate language and irony seem meant to make us
smile, if only somewhat bitterly.

Perhaps we find racial or ethnic controversy so
serious now that it does not seem much of a laughing
matter.

As you see from the headnote, I sometimes like to
follow up the discussion of expectation at the end of the
previous chapter with stop-and-go reading of this
selection.

## Gabrielle Roy
## WILHELM

Short story; French-Canadian and Dutch
As you will have noticed, the two "crossings" in the
first two selections in the chapter are not over great
stretches of ethnic water--Irish/Italian, both European,
both Catholic; French/Dutch, even closer neighbors in the
"Old Country," both Christian but one Catholic, the other
Protestant--and notice that the French Catholics and
Irish do get along well. (You might want to hark back to
Tony Ardizzone's story for another European mix--Italian
and Liechtensteiner.) These stories are set some sixty or
more years ago, but fences between such near neighbors
persisted at least until after World War II--and in some
measure still persist. I find it useful to begin this way
though it is in some measure, perhaps, political: to show
barriers that existed in living memory (though not in
our students' memories and only in that of the eldest of
us) but that now scarcely exist, is to suggest that what
are barriers now may not be so, or at least so high, a
half-century or less from now. So I like to ask right off
whether to the students or their parents or their
communities these "mini-barriers" still exist.

This piece seems an almost generic growing-up story
to me, and I like to ask about the first time each
student met someone from another culture (as Christine's
mother in "The Man from Mars" would say) and when the
world and the possibilities of becoming adult and knowing
that larger world seemed to open up. There is also the
somewhat cynical but tenderly handled generic "puppy
love" aspect here that might be worth talking about in
class. The narrator says in the first paragraph, "I
thought I loved Wilhelm," and that delicious youthful
sport of playing at love is begun. You might ask students
first to find all the clues they can to the narrator's
"real" feelings (or non-feelings), and then, if the time
is right, ask them to relate--perhaps in writing--a
similar experience in their far-off youth.

There is also a gender issue that could be raised:
"Here was the first man who, through me, could be made
happy or unhappy" (par. 1). Your students may want to

light into the implications of that one, of what gender roles were assumed, etc. The end of par. 3 may add some more fuel to the fire, as might the "chivalry" in par. 6.


Jeffery Paul Chan
THE CHINESE IN HAIFA

Short story; Chinese-American and Jewish-American
I sometimes ask students to imagine this story without its ethnic content; one of these days I might even ask them to write a summary of the story in which everybody in the story is an Anglo-American. This often shows up the centrality of the cultural context.

Such an exercise is useful here, for, despite the catchy title highlighting ethnicity, it is easy to see this story as simply another modern tale of modern suburban hanky-panky. If your class is somehow struck by or stuck at the "modernity" of the story--drugs and divorce and adultery--you may need to go the other way and ask them to underline all the ethnic details from the title to the final sentence.

In either case, we can start with the dream that opens the story. There the cultural theme seems very strong indeed. We have starving Asian children described in some detail, the "strangely familiar schoolyard" may suggest that Bill is translating them to America or that he somehow knows the school yard though it is far away; students argue for both readings and I cannot make up my mind, contenting myself with the near-oxymoron "strangely familiar" as almost emblematic of Bill's relation to his Chinese nature. The grandfather's door is Chinese and traditional, so that by attribution we assume the grandfather was or is too. Bill's father, however, when he appears is playing golf in American attire (and cheating--does this suggest his Americanization?!). In the second paragraph the fourth generation is introduced, Bill's children, who are learning to write Chinese. In some ways, it seems to me, the divorce is virtually the emblem of the struggle between cultural heritage and "Americanization," if it is not too provincial to call it that.

I cannot let the class leave the topic of heritage and change without getting to the conversation between Mrs. Greenberg and Bill, pars. 106-124. I bring up the stereotypical similarities between Chinese and Jews, 137-39, from which the story gets its title, and the "crossing" in the story through Bill's relations with Ethel. I want to draw from them some recognition that what the Jewish portion of the story does is to establish that there are other cultural heritages; i.e., that Bill and Ethel are not just stepping over the line of a heritage into heritagelessness but are coming together from two strongly influential "minority" cultures. It thus has the mark of "Americanization" in its crosscultural movement but not "Americanization" in the sense of moving from a minority to a majority culture.

### Paula Gunn Allen
### POCAHONTAS TO HER ENGLISH HUSBAND, JOHN ROLFE

Poem; Native American and English

I hope your students do a good job in reading this poem aloud for I find its strong and tender tone complex and very moving. There is a tone of profoundly wise acceptance in Pocahontas's voice: she understands Rolfe's racism, his feeling of superiority, yet can accept him—if not it—because of her sense of her own and her culture's worth, her own sense of security. I like to ask the class about the sentence that begins at the end of l. 16. Not only is it useful for helping to define tone, but think of all the ways (vengeful, mocking . . . ) she could have treated the irony of tobacco as the basis of wealth and death, I urge them. And before I leave the sentence, what about "other powers / than those you know"? I find students like to try to deduce the religious implications of the poem. But I try also to push them to infer a whole history of imperialism from it: not only the exploitation of the native population (though certainly that) and the well-known importation of disease, but especially the implied relationship between Rolfe and his "masters far across the sea" and his own ignorance of the world he inhabits ("my world through which you tumbled").

### Wendy Rose
### JULIA

Poem; Native American (Hopi)

There is a strange and striking similarity, I feel, between this poem and Paula Gunn Allen's Pocahontas poem. Besides the fact that both are written by Native American women, both poems are spoken by women to a beloved husband who feels or felt superior to them, both women are dead, and in both poems the time of speaking and of the events spoken about is complicated. Do your students find these poems at all similar? The grotesquerie and powerful pathos of the Rose poem overwhelms many of my students so that it is difficult for them to find any other poem comparable.

This, I find, is a good poem for reading aloud and a splendid one as well for "answering" in another poem or prose piece, though few students want to put themselves in the place of the husband. There might also be a good topic for discussion or a personal essay in lines 19-29: how do we see ourselves in the dark? I get rather heated discussion sometimes on the subject of appearance and identity. Who are you? What is the relationship between the way you look and what you really are? Isn't Julia beautiful "on the inside"? Would you (if male) want to marry her? Surely not? Is it really possible to separate appearance and identity? Don't you become or aren't you affected by your appearance? And doesn't "ugliness" or "deformity" at times repel or lessen others' attraction: have any of the attractive women students or the athletic males found that they were not taken seriously as students or deeply thinking, feeling people?

Comparing Julia and Katherine Anne Porter's Ottilie might make for an interesting but rather touchy discussion. I haven't tried it yet, so if you do, let me know whether I should.


### Gary Soto
### LIKE MEXICANS

Nonfiction; Chicano and Japanese-American

Sometimes I like to begin with grandparents' advice (I usually lie and say my grandfather, a tire distributor, told me as I was going off to college to be sure to study handwriting and spelling because he couldn't read anything any of those college boys wrote for him and when he could he found they had misspelled even the simple words. It is a lie because it wasn't my grandfather--it was my uncle.). But if I've had too much chit-chat about families and personal experiences, I start with expectations: What expectations does the title arouse? When the grandmother advises him not to marry an Okie, what do you expect will happen? I ask. And I ask these questions again when, in par. 4, the speaker tells his friend Scott that he will never marry an Okie. (If I decide my approach in time, I have the title, then the first paragraph, and then the first four paragraphs read in class before I assign the whole piece for reading at home. Of course, the wise students will know from the chapter that there has to be some "crossing," but that's all the more reason the later events may take them by surprise.)

The advice of family and friends to "marry poor" seems contrary to the conventional and somewhat cynical wisdom of the tribe: "It's just as easy to marry a rich _____ as a poor one." Are your students surprised by this advice? What do they make of it? Are any of your students offended by the poverty/untidiness of the Mexican and Japanese poor? Do they find it a hostile stereotype?

Alice Childress
WEDDING BAND

Play; Black and white

After the students have read the first scene, I ask
them to return to the stage directions and the sentence,
"The playing area of the houses are raised platforms
furnished according to the taste of each tenant", and try
to design the set to fit that description. I have
sometimes found some initial difficulty in keeping the
characters in supporting roles--in this play and in
others--straight. So I spend a little time going over or
distinguishing them. I especially want to have them
document Fanny's "middle-class" values, her four-piece,
silver-plated tea service that is "The first and only one
to be owned by a colored woman in the United States of
America," and even her "genuine, full-blooded, qualified,
Seminole Indian mother." I sometimes ask them to follow
up the characerization of Fanny throughout the play, and
ask them to discuss how this characterization prepares
them for the relative congeniality of Fanny's meeting
with Herman's mother. I use Fanny to try to illuminate
how much there is in this play about class, how it
interacts with the clash of race, and how both define the
"politics" of the play. My students are not too strong on
class or on the concept of class conflict, but it seems
one of the underlying themes of this moving, personal,
humane, but not apolitical play.

I usually have to call attention to the date--1918--
and am occasionally astounded, when I start drawing out
the references to the war, to find there is a good deal
of fuzziness about which World War was which. I also have
to supply some background on miscegenation laws and
miscegenation as a concept. You might want to check on
what particular barriers to marriage between ethnic
groups there were in your state or region, because in
many states, I know, the laws did not prohibit just white
and black marriages.

Before I get too deeply into the war and its
pervasive atmosphere in the play, I use my stop-and-go
reading gambit again. I ask them, before they get past
the first scene, what they expect to happen between
Nelson and Julia (see study question 4) and what
October's letter may foreshadow (see study question 6),
that is, the notion that Herman and Julia must separate
because Herman cannot offer her "his name and his
protection." Sometimes what I find is that a number of
students anticipate that Nelson will be the hero and
"rescue" Julia from her uncomfortable situation. It helps
that he is a soldier, but sometimes, if I probe enough,
and in the right way, I can bring to the surface the fact
that many (on both sides of the racial "fence") want the
play to end that way, that they--even this late in the

twentieth century--are as uneasy as the South Carolina lawmakers and public about interracial love and marriage. I can sometimes go on from here to talk about reader-response in terms of the reader's repertoire and prejudices or preconceptions, and how we sometimes read into a work our hopes as expectations. This also may be the point at which to talk about evaluation. What are the advantages and disadvantages of having our hopes fulfilled (even when expectations have been aroused which threaten a different ending)? What does it mean to have our hopes modified? radically changed? disappointed? I try not to disclose my Romantic assumptions that a text should be "new," that it should change the reader's perceptions, perhaps more, but it is difficult for me to escape my own vantage point and limitations.

Since a great deal of the power of this play depends on our recognition and acceptance of the love between Julia and Herman as real and deep and lasting, it sometimes seems necessary to ask students to find all of the details they can in the play to substantiate the love. (If there is some cogent opposition, that side should draw evidence from the play as well--one could do worse than have a debate on the issue.) I often ask students to compare the celebration of Julia's and Herman's tenth "wedding anniversary" in act I, scene 2, with that powerful confrontation between then in act II, scene 2 (my favorite) and use these two scenes to define the power of their love and the power of the forces arraigned against them.

I don't like to leave discussion of the play without doing at least a little with Herman's mother and, in particular, his sister. I try to bring out how some of the forces that prevent the marriage of Julia and Herman and the friendly relationship between the races also limit their lives. Despite the mother's role as virtual villain and her sometimes ugly hostility toward Julia, it seems to me she is treated sympathetically, as the agent rather than the origin of the racism of the time and place, and the economic victim of the same powers that reinforce the racism. It is easier to see the economic/class victimization of the sister, so I usually start with her and only then go on to Herman's mother.

<br>

nila northSun
**WHAT GRAMMA SAID ABOUT HER GRANDPA**

Poem; Native American (Shoshone-Chippewa) and European-American

I have found that though the antecedent of "Her" in the title is clearly "Gramma," there are some students who think it is the poet and that the poem is about the poet's Gramma and Grandpa rather than her grandmother and great-great-grandfather.

This little poem is useful to illustrate how we can sometimes understand more than the speaker seems to understand: most of us are probably rather indignant about Jim Butler's desertion of his Native American family. But the same details can also be used to show how the grandmother's accepting nature (is it stoic or sweet?) comes through her speech. And these details also reveal the nature of racism and its effect on both sides of the barrier. That a brief poem like this can be approached at least these three ways, all three of them appearing to be central or significant, may also suggest something about how literature works or how paraphrase is often powerless to catch a poem's import. (If you want to use a word like "overdetermined," this may be a good time to introduce it.)

## Gogisgi
## SONG OF THE BREED

Poem; Native American (Cherokee and mixed)
Why is this poem in "Crossing"? I ask this to get on the table the fact that "breed" means half-breed, more specifically, Native American and European-American. The speaker is, then, already "crossed." The chapter that began with rejection of a near-kin (Irish-Italian) outsider in "The Coming-Out of Maggie" ends with pieces having to do with the results of crossing in courtship and marriage, children with "mixed" heritage. Of course there are many other works in the text with mixed heritage--e.g., Tony Ardizzone's and Saul Bellow's stories in chapter 2 and Linda Hogan's and Joseph Bruchac's poems in chapter 3.

## Cyn. Zarco
## FLIPOCHINOS

Poem; Filipino-American and Chinese-American
You're on your own with this one--and watch your step.

## Barbara Thompson
## CROSSING

Short story; American and Pakistani
Since two of Barbara Thompson's stories (including "Crossing") have won Pushcart Prizes, I cannot claim literally to have "discovered" her. But she does not have a volume published yet and is not anthologized, so I do

have a kind of proprietary interest in this story. It is one of my favorites, and I am not likely to be very disinterested or judicious in teaching it or in suggesting how others teach it.

The two major elements I attack in class are expectation and theme, but first I dwell on the opening paragraphs. The first word of the story virtually establishes the setting, and before the paragraph is over we know that it is early afternoon on a Friday in April in the early 1970s in a western household in Lahore, Pakistan, and that the center of the story is likely to be Anne, who, in the first words of the second paragraph is identified as an American who has lived in Pakistan for twelve years. The third and fourth paragraphs suggest that Anne wants to hide from her husband the phone call from Libby, and that the three women--Anne, Libby, and the young Pakistani servant girl are "sisters" in the conspiracy against "the hegemony of men."

I then try to glide gracefully into expectation and suspense (though I find I must inform my students that there was no Soviet military presence in Afghanistan in the early 1970s , so it's probably not going to be a Cold War or spy story). What do we know by the end of the telephone conversation? I ask coyly, and hope (or insist) that we get on the table a clear understanding of the situation. Anne and Libby are going to take their sons-- Sheriyar and Masood (the only two mentioned in this conversation)--across the border into Afghanistan, that Libby's son Masood is crossing secretly ("'No one even knows about you and Masood,' Anne says"), and, at the very end of the passage, where we must pause an extra millisecond because of the white space beyond, Anne hears a man's laughter from Libby's end of the line (after she has said she is at "a friend's flat").

It isn't hard to follow the adventure plot from this point on, noting what we learn as we go along, holding our breath at the border, and so on to the end of the story. But I don't stop there. What are our expectations now? <u>Will</u> Libby show up? Will Anne lose her son Sheriyar because of her complicity in the "kidnapping," the violation of the Pakistani male "rights" to his male children? I think there's a good chance this will happen; despite Iqbal's tolerance of western ways, his honor and his position in the (male-dominated) community is compromised.

But just to show you how unauthoritative that view is, I have it from the author that she thinks Anne will show. Who is right? This might serve as an instance where you can ask the question about the "ownership" or authority of authors. <u>Is</u> the author privileged in interpreting the work or in on "inside information" that is not in the text? Or, once published, does a work become the reader's (or the reading public's), and is the authority then the text plus the reader? This issue is brought up in a more acceptable way in the afterword, where the topic is the articulation of a story's theme, but here we're talking about "fact," or at least inference.

If I haven't lost your trust by this time, let me just say I now go on to theme, and you can see how I handle it by reading the afterword again, where I use this story to illustrate my discussion of theme.

## IN THE AMERICAN SOCIETY

The afterword takes up in some detail, questions about context. The selections here tend to make substantial demands on readers to supply information from outside the text of individual selections. Footnotes help, of course, and we have provided them when we have thought them to be absolutely necessary, but the really crucial points about referentiality cannot be provided in a line or two explaining a particularity. It is a good idea, in constructing writing assignments, to go with the selections here and to provide reasons (or at least excuses) for students to have to use the library to find out particular things. The idea of contextual needs is, finally, pretty subtle; people don't quite know they <u>need</u> contextual knowledge until they already have it and discover that they are applying it in a particular way that affects interpretation of the text.

One way to get students to thinking about contexts is to return again to an issue that we raised in the text in chapter 1, and that you may well have built into your course early on, namely, the question of setting. If you have not said much about setting in teaching selections from later chapters, I suggest you return to issues of setting in an emphatic way in teaching the first few selections in this chapter. Physical setting is, in one way or another, important to almost all the selections, and it is almost always healthy to go over such a basic element in stories; often in poems, too. But temporal setting, always harder to teach, is a kind of transition to context. If you can get your students thinking about time and history in relation to what actually happens with the text, you can more readily get them to accept the idea of going beyond the text, even before they go <u>to</u> it, so to speak. Temporal setting, then, leads almost imperceptibly to issues of context, and you can make the transition here to a whole new dimension of writing--the historical and cultural one--while seeming just to go back and review one of the most basic "elements" of writing.

Gish Jen
IN THE AMERICAN SOCIETY

Short story; Chinese-American

Begin with setting. Setting here is simple, in a way, but gets complicated as the scene changes. Get your students to fill out the details of the party scene especially, but lead up to that through simple recounting of what the pancake house seems to look like. A related way to move into the central issues of the story is through the material objects important to individual characters--the suit to the father, of course, and the bottle to Jeremy--but various material symbols to the narrator and mother too. They merge with setting in the symbolism of the country club and in the way things go "swimmingly" (as the narrator says) there. What things represent to individuals and what places mean to them are important to the conflict of values: you can get at almost everything in the story through setting and things (almost everything, that is, except dialogue; and I do think it is a good idea, because the dialogue is so good, to pause over the way people are so carefully characterized here by what they say and how they say it).

Nicholas Gerros
GREEK HORATIO ALGER

Interview; Greek-American

The tone of this selection is very interesting to contrast with that of the Jen story above. Your students may want to argue about whether the differences in tone result from the choice of point of view--how would a daughter view Gerros's values as presented here and what would _her_ tone be?--or from differences involved in the cultural context. Context will, in any case, come up almost automatically here, and the way to make a discussion of it meaningful is to get the students to put this account firmly into a temporal setting.

Your students may want to argue about Algerian (that is, Horatio Algerian) values relative to the American Dream. Let them. The opinions they begin with will have a lot to do with how they respond to Gerros initially and perhaps even ultimately. But then get them to talk about the father in the Jen story in relation to Algerian values. If they respond differently to that story-- finding, for example, the Jen father to be, though comic, attractive and Gerros too materialistic--get them to account for the differences in terms of the way the two men are _presented_.

Jimmy Santiago Baca
SO MEXICANS ARE TAKING JOBS FROM AMERICANS

Poem; Chicano
The study questions here will set your students up
to discuss the way the poem creates a metaphor out of an
idiomatic expression (but the questions just put the
issue in terms of vividness; you can supply the notion of
metaphor). The questions also will set up a discussion
of values.


Mari Evans
THE FRIDAY LADIES OF THE PAY ENVELOPE

Poem; Afro-American
This is probably the poem to use to recall earlier
issues of setting and extend them to context. I would
begin, however, with questions about how the "ladies" are
characterized, and get students to detail how Evans uses
language to control readers' feelings toward the ladies.
To get students to care about contextual issues, you
might ask them what they would ideally like to know about
<u>when</u> and <u>why</u> Evans wrote this poem.


Toni Cade Bambara
THE LESSON

Short story; Afro-American
If you did not spend much time on dialogue in Jen's
"In the American Society," by all means do it here. Bring
in the Jen story for comparison: both stories are
brilliant at capturing speech rhythms, both characterize
their people mainly through their uses of language, and
both have carefully thought out views of human nature
that are expressed through their sense of humor. One way
to begin is simply to get students talking about what
they find funny in the story. And why. The way to get a
discussion of setting going here--a discussion which can
merge into a discussion of context--is to ask them what
the Fifth Avenue setting <u>represents</u>--to Miss Moore, to
the students, and to readers.


Richard Dokey
SANCHEZ

Short story; Chicano
I like to teach this story as an exercise in
clarifying generational values. Get your students to
detail how they feel about the main characters and how
their feelings change in the course of the story. Make


In the American Society / 100

them support their evaluations by detailed references to the text. Get them to be clear about Juan's values and the values supported in the text.

Structure is also a good thing to review in teaching this story. The story covers a lot of ground, spatially and temporally, yet keeps a tight rein on plot.

## Bharati Mukherjee
## HINDUS

Short story; Indian-American

Detailing the new world/old world contrasts in this story may be the best way to begin class discussion. Such a discussion of contrasts leads quickly to a discussion of the narrator—which I would put off as long as you can because it can create a bit of dramatic structure for your class—and to a growing sense of complication among worlds. Your students may feel they need to know more about classes and castes in Indian society. Good; it will lead them to worry about contexts and what they need to know. Ultimately, have the class discuss in some detail how they feel about the narrator. It is probably best to hold until last a discussion of her values and where they come from; this discussion will take you back to the new world/old world distinctions.

## Linda Hogan
## BLACK HILLS SURVIVAL GATHERING, 1980

Poem; Native American (Chickasaw)

Beginning with the title has several advantages for class discussion. In the first place, "Black Hills" leads quickly to a consideration of geographical setting and then "1980" defines the temporal setting involving the larger cultural situation behind the poem's occasion. Both the other words of the title are important and resonant, too, and much of the poem can be gotten at through a discussion of their implications. Why is "gathering" important and what does it imply (community, common values, the bringing together of disparate individuals into a whole)? What various senses of survival are important to the poem? (The study questions will set up this discussion for you)

Another feature of the poem worth class time involves its organization and narrative aspects. In several ways, the poem organizes itself much as a short story would, with setting, exposition, characterization, and emerging conflict being important elements in its early arrangement. But unlike a story, it simply presents and doesn't resolve, leaving its emphasis on the situation and appropriate emotional responses to it. You can get a good discussion going about what would have to happen next to make the "plot" here work as a story. You might even have students "finish" the story as a story, and discuss how different endings lead to effects entirely different from those generated by this poem. Because of its "story" and its closeness, up to a point, to the narrative mode, it is an especially useful text for making generic or modal distinctions. Of course you can also stick to strictly thematic considerations and note how its presentation of ideas and values is just as complex as that in stories or plays in which the potential destruction of family or community life is an issue.

## Clark Blaise
## A CLASS OF NEW CANADIANS

Short story; Canadian and mixed

This is a good story to use to return to a discussion of character. I like to get students first of all to review elements of characterization here that we have talked about in other stories. Begin with one or two of the "type" characters, and have the students show which details establish quickly not only what each person is like but what function he or she performs in the story. But then move quickly to Dyer, and go over in some detail just how many different ways we learn about him.

The essential "move" here is to get from traditional characterization to questions of how Dyer becomes representative of something larger than himself--how he becomes (rather than comes from, as the minor characters do) some larger cultural "type." One way of thinking about the story is, in fact, to consider how Blaise sets out to define a "new" type. To get to this issue you will need to begin to fold into the discussion questions about how life in Montreal is represented, what kind of cultural values Dyer has, why and in what exact ways he feels at home in Montreal, and how he differs (although a transient himself) from the transient students he encounters. You can readily distill this set of issues from the title. (Do you get the idea that this is one of my favorite devices? My only defense is that it is also a favorite device for authors.) Ask whether the "new Canadians" phrase applies to Dyer as well as to the students. Ask exactly how his newness is different. Then ask about "class" and get them to explore the ambiguities in the word once the story begins to develop.

Norma Rosen
A THOUSAND TEARS

Short story; Puerto Rican and European-American
    If you taught <u>West</u> <u>Side</u> <u>Story</u> earlier in the course,
it may be worth reminding your students of some of the
issues you discussed in it at the same time you assign "A
Thousand Tears." The cultural and temporal backdrop are
roughly the same here, except that this story is told
from the guilt-ridden, liberal perspective of someone on
the outside of the issue but who is a still a neighbor.
It is worth spending a lot of time on sorting out just
what Sandra Loeb feels and what she conceives her
relationship to the neighborhood to be.  The details of
her expedition into the street and her careful--almost
too careful--decisions about which story to go in when
she is clad in a particular way are worth as much time in
class as the more dramatic episodes in which hostile
neighbors comment crudely on Puerto Rican behavior.
    There are at least two ways to read the emphases of
this story--as a story about marriage or as a story about
neighborhoods.  Ultimately, of course, the two parts come
together neatly, and you may wish to spend some time on
the husband's character since it is presented so much
more obliquely than that of Sandra Loeb.  But you may
find--as I have--that students are much less interested
(unless you have a group of "older"--that is beyond
teens--students in your class) in the marriage part of
the story.  Most younger students respond more readily to
the urban neighborhood issues; you can quickly get to the
center of them by doing character analysis on Sandra Loeb
and then on the "two" Puerto Ricos (the island and the
community in New York), actually treating the idea of
Puerto Rico as the story presents it as "character." You
may need to supply more of the marriage theme in the
story yourself, or at least question hard to get them to
confront the relationship issue implicit in the
anniversary scene and in questions of faded memory.


Pat Mora
IMMIGRANTS

Poem; Immigrant-American
    One way to get at tone--perhaps the most complex
issue to solve here--is to look at the fact that
"American" is capitalized in the first line but not in
the last two.  Another element of contrast that may help
your students understand the subtle way attitude is
expressed involves the growing darkness in the poem; from
happy, cheerful, mindless advice at the beginning, the
speaker moves to whispers and dark fears from l. 9 on.
You <u>may</u> be able to get at tone and attitude through a

In the American Society / 103

discussion of speaker, too, though your students will need to have developed a certain sophistication and subtlety for this strategy to work in class.

In fact, "speaker" may ultimately <u>not</u> be the proper concept to use in interpreting the poem. With a really good group of students, I like to get them considering the question of speaker, and they often come to the conclusion that the poet uses a sarcastic <u>stance</u> that finally is rather different from the consistent figure implied by the term speaker. Irony, then, may be as good a way of getting to the central issues of attitude and stance as through the concept of speaker itself. But whether you think "speaker" explains the poem fully enough--or whether you wish to develop in discussion a more sophisticated concept of stance and irony--you can thrust students into the midst of the issue by having them describe the advantage of casting the poem entirely in the imperative mood and cloaking its critical message as simple "advice."

This poem always reminds me of Marge Piercy's fine poem "Barbie Doll," and if you are looking for ways to move students out of the textbook and into the library-- or for ways of making reading or writing connections beyond the classroom, you might suggest that they dig that poem out of the library or bring it into class yourself for comparison. Both poems, by using such seemingly "unpoetic" images of popular culture, challenge some prevailing notions that students often have about what material is proper for poetic treatment.


Mitsuye Yamada
THE QUESTION OF LOYALTY

Poem; Japanese-American

This poem is useful to compare with Okita's poem about relocation centers, though its tone and methods are very different. It can provide a good example for showing students how very different kinds of poems can be made from similar materials and thematic interests. The speaker here is worth a good bit of classroom analysis, and the question of what students come to think of the speaker may be easiest to approach through a comparison with the speaker in the Okita poem.


Martin Luther King, Jr.
I HAVE A DREAM

Speech; Afro-American

For some students, the content here will be so familiar that they may be startled to see it written down. The words do, somehow, seem a little distant when presented as a text rather than as a clip from a news broadcast or part of a video presentation. This feeling can present an opportunity to get students involved in contextual issues by asking them to draw on their memories and inquiring about what sense of audience, context, and history they feel they need to understand the text appropriately. I like to remind students of oral texts we have read earlier and invite them to notice what features these texts have in common that differ from written texts. Get them to isolate, here, the various oral strategies--the repetition, the echoing of earlier phrases, and structures, etc.--but insist that they notice, too, the way the speech allusively draws on traditional materials, a strategy we usually associate (quite wrongly) with written texts. Ask your students how much of the speech makes sense without a knowledge of Lincoln and the Bible. Ask them how much history they have to know to respond appropriately. Ask them in what sense the speech draws on assumptions about how a "live" audience might respond, becoming "one" with the speaker as the speech goes on.


Luis Valdez
THE SHRUNKEN HEAD OF PANCHO VILLA

Play; Chicano
     Context is a crucial issue for discussion here. Many of your students may need a substantial history lesson-- which is best administered outside of and before class discussion--to get the drift of the play.  I ask students to read, at least one class in advance of assigning this play, about Pancho Villa in the library, and in a class prior to teaching the play itself we have some discussion of his life and what he represents symbolically in Mexican history.  Trying to "explain" history as one goes along through the play is difficult, and students are apt to lose interest in the play quickly if they begin it without a full sense of Villa's mythic significance.
     The biggest onstage issue here involves the head. Some students, in my experience, are very put off by the ugliness of the image, and it is probably best to confront this issue--inevitably--head on by asking students just what the visual metaphor accomplishes.  You might sneak up on the issue by getting them to talk about how they would "stage" the bodiless head, then ask them why the playwright uses such a dramatic unattractive device.
     This discussion may be the place, too, to take up another controversial issue; the question of the play's language which, for many students, seems too earthy and unnecessarily crude.  Get them to talk about the reason behind the deliberate crudeness, to defend the

author's decision to have the head fart on stage and the
deliberate drawing on bathroom jokes and locker-room
humor.  Ask them what the tradeoffs are, here, for the
risk of disgusting an audience.  Ask them where their
sympathies go if they become disturbed by the crudeness.

The play has a lively stage quality, and you may
need to remind students of that--especially if they have not
seen many plays or if you have not had a chance to deal
with videos, films, or stage performances in class--by
doing some scenes in class (be prepared for "actors" to
be embarrassed by the lines they have to deliver) or by
asking them how they would stage, visually, the character
of Mingo.

Helena Maria Viramontes
THE MOTHS

Short story; Chicana
     I have difficulty, I confess, in dealing with
fictions that introduce supernatural elements into the
literal world of the fiction. I am leary of elements that
I cannot explain away psychologically or as the
perspective of a character not necessarily endorsed by
the fiction as a whole, and of elements that are fanciful
or self-consciously fictional or arbitrary. Though some
of my students have less trouble than I (I explain this
to myself by thinking it's because they do not take
fiction as seriously in the first place), there are
enough who share my naturalistic, skeptical outlook to
make it worthwhile to explore the supernatural or surreal
in a work. Here, for example, I begin with the potato
slices that the speaker's grandmother put on the girl's
temples to treat her scarlet fever. Did the cure work?
Does the story affirm the efficacy of the treatment?
Well, then, it <u>could be</u> that this is just a bit of folk
superstition, meant to characterize the grandmother and
her world rather than the world of the story. Not too
many students will take the opposite view here without
citing other things in the story, which I forbid at this
point. Still, I want to let it hang there--it's probably
a superstition unendorsed by the story--you don't <u>have</u> to
believe it (in the sense of accepting it as part of the
literal world or belief of the fiction) . . . but you
can, that's the point; you don't have to, but you can.
     The speaker was skeptical too, so her already
oversized hands began to grow, until Abuelita made the
swelling go down with a balm made of dry moth wings. So
the speaker, who was as skeptical as we, is convinced.
But are we? Do we really believe her hands grew huge? Or
was it the imagination of the girl under the influence of
her grandmother's superstition? And what do we do with
the dry moth wings? Surely in reading a story called "The
Moths" we'd notice this even as early as the third
paragraph. My students feel an almost irresistible
tendency to start talking at this point about symbols--
the moths are symbols. What this means, I usually find,
is that if a student can identify something as a symbol
he or she does not have to take it seriously or literally
as part of the "actual" world of the fiction.
     So I go on like that until we come to the final
appearance of the moths. Some will try to subsume this
scene into a naturalistic world by making the speaker an

unreliable narrator--we don't <u>have</u> to believe that she
saw the moths. But I try to discourage that, suggesting
that if we don't believe that she saw the moths, why
should we believe she was really there at all? or that
she ever had a grandmother? Still, there are those who
want to distance the story's reality from their own by
suggesting that the whole experience, so intense and
significant for the young girl, traumatizes her, and
induces visions like those the grandmother might have
had. One ambiguous phrase in the final paragraph--
"telling me about the moths that lay within the soul and
slowly eat the spirit up"--may suggest that the
grandmother had prepared her for this vision. I'd just as
soon leave it there, but you will probably have other
directions to take the whole discussion in.
     I don't like to concentrate solely on the
supernatural here, though I may give it more emphasis now
that I will be teaching it in its new context as the
first story in this chapter. There is a complementary
aspect to this story, an almost near-focus realism of
detail, like the exposition of the transplanting of roots
in par. 5 (see study question 5), the washing of the
grandmother's body, and the description of the body
itself. I like to ask students how they reconcile this
kind of detail--and the speaker keeping a brick in her
sock to hit her sisters with--with the almost mystic
tenderness and love of the rest of the story. Does the
realism anchor or affirm the surreal, that is, does the
speaker make us believe her through her use of realistic
details?
     And finally I pounce on this phrase in the last
paragraph, "feeling half born." What does that mean? How
can the death of her grandmother make her feel as if she
is in the process of being born? After a while, if it
doesn't come up, I slyly get them to look at paragraph 13
(not that I'm superstitious).


                    Toshio Mori
             ABALONE, ABALONE, ABALONE

Short story; Japanese-American
     Not all my students find this story as compelling or
hypnotic (like polishing abalone shells?) as I do. What
they say is that it's "weird." Exactly, I say, meaning
mysterious. Before I suggest that this may have something
to do with Taoism (about which I know very little) and
living apart from society and studying and meditating
upon nature, I first make sure they know what abalone, or
at least mother of pearl looks like. Then I try to get
them to describe just how the speaker gets hooked on abalo
shells and what it is he sees in them (I try to get them
back to pars. 9, 16, and 17). Finally, I say something

like, Okay, so abalone shells are beautiful, but aren't two or three enough? Why pile up more and more and more? Someone's sure to hit back with par. 28--alike and different. If I'm lucky we get to talking about how generalizations and classifications tend to erase distinctions, but that, in reality, every individual leaf, shell, fingerprint, snowflake, person, is different--they're like other leaves, shells, fingerprints, snowflakes, and people, only different. My students like to talk about things like that. It's cheating, I know, but I have no scruples when it comes to getting them to read, and talk about and write about what they read, especially when they find it meaningful, serious, and exciting.

Walter Lew<br>LEAVING SEOUL: 1953

Poem; Korean-American
   I find this poem intensely interesting, moving . . . and puzzling. I'm not even sure what it says much less what it means. I haven't taught it yet, but I'm planning to as soon as this book is published, hoping that my students will be able to explain bits of it to me. (I like to use a few pieces that I have not come to terms with and throw them out to a class admitting my puzzlement. I think it salutary to reveal to students that we lofty profs don't know everything about literature [they know we don't know much about a lot of other things that interest them], that a couple dozen heads are better than one, that literature is open to multiple reading, and that enjoyment and admiration can at times precede full understanding. Of course we can't get away with faking it too often, pretending not to understand something we think we do. And we can't teach too many things that puzzle us or the Dean will hear about it.)
   Let me start with the last word of the poem--see how turned around I am? I assume "hers" means "her urn." One of the tall glowing jars in the poem's present contains her ashes. Who is the father in the last line? The speaker's father? Why would the jars contents (presumably one of them contains the father's ashes), give him dominion over her or over her ashes? What do they contain that gives him dominion? I don't think the father is the speaker's father, rather the speaker's father's father, the one who, decades ago is spoken of as lost (l. 18). And so I assume that it is the father's--i.e., the grandfather's--urn, along with (what?) others being buried in 1953. Which makes me read the poem as saying that the need to revere parents and forebears gives them power (dominion) over us, and gives us a morality, duty,

and so on. So I go back to 1. 1 and emphasize the auxiliary verb: "We <u>have</u> <u>to</u> bury the urns." But you may have a better idea.

(Another way of getting at all this, rather than beginning with "hers," is to begin with that first line and ask why they have to bury the urns.)

If it suits your purposes at this point in the course, you can avoid the explication to some extent by making a good writing assignment out of this poem. The scene here almost reminds me of the final scene in <u>Casablanca</u> (but lots of things remind me of <u>Casablanca</u>), so I'm tempted to ask students to write a movie script or story based on this scene, filling in as much as they can of the background (the mother is a doctor, the father is wearing a discarded U. S. Army coat, hatless, smoking a Lucky Strike). What's going on? Why do they have to bury the urns? What's in them? What's the hurry?

<br>

### N. Scott Momaday
### THE EAGLE-FEATHER FAN

Poem; Native American (Kiowa)

I first look for a very simple summary from the students of what the speaker says is happening (he is probably dancing to the music, the singing, and the drums, and is certainly holding a fan made of eagle feathers. He says the fan is actually an eagle which takes off with his hand that has become part of the eagle-fan and soared in the heavens over the mountains). Being as literal-minded as I am (see guide discussion of "The Moths"), I want to ask students first to describe what is <u>really</u> going on here. This soon leads to a discussion of subjective versus objective reality, and, if I'm not careful, or if I am in the mood, into Thomas Kuhn's subjective paradigm and the recognition that science, too, is species(human)-specific and not about what is "out there" the way we used to think it was. You can see how I return to the poem by the last portions of the second study questions. Regardless of what you believe is real and what is "only imaginary," you can at least appreciate the point of view of the dancer/speaker and recognize that there are other ways of looking at the universe and at reality than yours or the conventional way. You don't have to believe in the other reality to appreciate someone else's perspective. This seems to me a cardinal aesthetic principle (and, interestingly enough, an ethical/moral one as well).

Garrison Keillor
PROTESTANT

Short story; Scandinavian-American

It may be necessary to deal with the third study question first: religion and humor do not mix very well in American public life at times. If your class is particularly sensitive, you may want to turn the abstraction lever up a notch and guide the discussion into the frequent tendency of highly principled organizations--religious, political, or social--to splinter on narrower and narrower grounds. We do not do this very much in American public life: the Democratic and Republican parties, for example, are very broad and overlapping. Some would say, therefore, they do not really stand for _anything_. Would it be better to have more parties with firmer, if narrower principles? Cardinal Newman, who left the Anglican Church for Roman Catholicism, somewhere said that Anglicans can believe almost anything--but of course they never do! Some such discussion of compromise, coalition, or principle might dampen forever some fireworks--if you want them dampened. (You might point out that "Protestant" suggests "protesting" as well as naming a church.)

You are, of course, the best judge as to whether this is the right way to start your class discussion: it may or may not be necessary. It is not raised until the third study question in the text because we did not want such issues to overwhelm the consideration of Keillor's warmly funny piece; so we started with humor. It's very difficult to explain why something is funny, but it does seem necessary to advise the solemn youths in your class that a piece actually read for an assignment can be funny.

Keillor can be very subtle or quiet, so sometimes you may need to turn up the volume. The beginning of paragraph 3 both raises the blasphemy issue and illustrates Keillor's humorous twists: "Jesus said, 'Where two or three are gathered together in my name, there am I in the midst of them,' and the Brethren believed that was enough." Christ's words are not being made fun of, but the Brethren's demand that only those whose beliefs were "pure," that is, identical, doomed them to very small congregations and they thought that enough, perhaps even proof of their purity. Even that belief is not being made fun of; it is the result, the tiny congregation, that is shown as somehow ludicrous (at least to those who think of congregations as large gatherings). There is no overt scoffing at the purist positions decribed in the paragraph, but the five sentences beginning with "No" give the impression that the Brethren's purity was more a matter of negation and denial than of positive and joyous belief. Perhaps the total seriousness, the spare, severe rigors of their faith, and the absence of joy are what seem to require some humor or joy in their description to balance the picture.

What may make this seem difficult to understand for our students is our generally hedonistic culture; the Brethren might seem to them "kooks" or masochists. The almost wistful respect for such honest self-denial in Keillor's tone that must be appreciated to make the whole piece both funny and moving may be lost. It's up to us to make sure it isn't.

Durango Mendoza
SUMMER WATER AND SHIRLEY

Short story; Native American (Creek)

My classes want to know if the story affirms the belief in witchcraft and the like that the first-person narrator seems to believe in. It may be wise to begin by having the class compile all the apparent evidence and line it up with the counterstatements: the timing of Shirley's fever is a coincidence; the communal "superstitions," reinforced by the brother's recent behavior and the fever make Shirley believe she sees the "three little men" (par. 35); her vision and his own belief make him think he sees the yellow dog with the brown spots that he is apparently "supposed to see" if Shirley is indeed cursed; he and his mother only think they smell the hot monstrous flesh and hear the yellow dog's nails (par. 55)--after all, they see nothing; the doctor, finds nothing wrong with her; we have no confirmation other than the boy's superstition-filled mind that there was an evil smell in the room that receded when he touched the wet pebbles (par. 71); and the boy's prayers and force of will only precede the rain, they do not cause it. That may seem like an awful lot of explaining away, and a little bit too much skepticism about the details of the story. This may be a good time to talk about point of view and the fact that almost all the explanations are primarily one explanation: we only have the boy's perceptions and report for most of the evidence and a little more from the community whose beliefs he shares. For the skeptical, the "clincher" may be that Shirley, before she gets sick and superstitious too, points out that their mother told them stiginees never have to go to the toilet and Ansul Middlecreek is coming from the outhouse when they first see him (par. 19).

All this, in my class, leads up to the question of what difference it makes. The story is essentially the experience of Sonny; the beliefs are the means by which he comes to terms with his experience, they are indeed the experience itself. If literature has as one of its functions at least the ability to take us almost out of ourselves and our way of looking at things into another different way of seeing, then this story, if it works for us, is a successful piece of literature. In addition, I like to suggest, a story with another way of seeing of which we might be skeptical may suggest that we reexamine the grounds of our own beliefs and our own way of experiencing. It may make us more self-conscious, more aware of the way belief conditions what we think of as reality.

Rafael Jesús González
SESTINA: SANTA PRISCA

Poem; Chicano
I first go through this highly visual, highly wrought poem image by image and sentence by sentence. I insist that students look up all the uncommon words--like "chasuble" and "vellum" and "phylacteries"--for the sense, of course, and also to show how intricately the words and images are entwined. I then get them literally to draw pictures of the saints ("gesticulating" I remind them) and of as much of the church as they can. <u>Then</u> I go into more detail about the sestina form and how the sentence endings all come so neatly at the ends of the lines. My students are astounded and sometimes excited by what they find. This is clearly a poem that is deliberately intricate--though not necessarily therefore deliberately difficult. I think this a wonderful poem, but I have to caution my class that though the elaborate (baroque) form works well and is admirable, not <u>all</u> wonderful poems need be so self-consciously and intricately constructed. This is marvelous of its kind, but is not the only kind. I do not want to sound negative, because I like this poem, but I don't want to lead my class to what I believe are mistaken notions of the nature of poetry in showing up the very real splendors of this particular work.

Audre Lorde
REINS

Poem; Caribbean-American (Carriacou)
There is no way I can keep my students who know or learn that Audre Lorde's family is from the West Indies from assuming that this poem is based on West Indian lore. Should I? I don't like to impose, or have students impose, biographical grids onto literary works. But, then, why do I attach headnotes with biographical information? I use this poem to introduce the topic of

biography and text, author and speaker. (We all have our own versions of how this should go, so no need to go through that here.)

I do ask them to resist the biographical impulse, just to exercise their imagination and their sense of detail in reconstructing the kind of country from which this advice to the pregnant and nursing may have come. Animals, fish, streams, rabbits, coconuts, and a society with spirits that can harm or even kill children, and the desire for many children. Hmmmm.

If I don't wander off on biography I touch on the same issue I do in teaching the Mendoza story--the non-condescending sharing of a vision not our own as one of the pleasures and purposes of literature.


## Ishmael Reed
### I AM A COWBOY IN THE BOAT OF RA

Poem; Afro-American

As I do with the González poem, I go through this elaborate work virtually line by line. I know it's difficult to explain a joke, but I have to point out some of the playfulness at first because so many of my students think all poetry (except limericks) Highly Serious. I let study questions 1 and 2 do some of the work and finally get Set for (it's contagious) the final verse-paragraph.

The fusion of the cowboy and the African myths tickles me, but I realize they are also serious. I see this poem not only as a celebration of blackness and its demand for equal status with myths of the American West, but also as an emblem of the mixed heritage of the Afro-American Afro-American, and I sometimes compare it to Countee Cullen's "Heritage," for all the differences in tone and attitude.


## Cynthia Ozick
### BLOODSHED

Short story; Jewish-American

I find it necessary at times to give a sketchy context for this story, seeking the help of any Jewish students who might be in the class. In my simplified version, I suggest that American Jews fifty years ago were pretty well assimilated into American society. They were mostly the children or grandchildren of immigrants, and the Old Country, along with Yiddish and strict religious observance, was fading from the majority. With Hitler and the horror of the Holocaust, many American Jews were reawakened to their ethnic identity and with it, in many cases, to their religion. Ethnic identity and pride were reinforced by the founding of the Jewish state in Israel after World War II. When survivors of the death camps came into this country in large numbers after that war, in many quarters there was a sense of guilt: at having had it easy while millions were being slaughtered, at having loosened ties of nationality and faith while so many coreligionists were dying simply because they were ethnic Jews, and so on. As a result, there was not only a revival of Judaism in America but a burgeoning fundamentalism: a strict Old Testament, literalist, almost Puritan and mystical Hasidism. (I try to relate this to the worldwide fundamentalist movement in recent decades in America, the Arabic states, and elsewhere.) In this story, then, the more typical Americanized Jew of the mid-century visits a female relative who was once like him but has now married into the Hasidic community. In this context I then return to the details of the story. (We seriously considered at one point putting this story in chapter 6, "The Man from Mars," for there is here a confrontation not just of people and ideas but virtually of worlds. We chose to put it here because the religious emphasis is so strong, but it could be taught with profit in the earlier chapter.)

The first 16 or 18 paragraphs of the story introduce Bleilip and us to the commune. I sometimes lead the students through the beginning inviting them to ask questions about the details. The first place I zero in on is the conversation with Toby and her new life, his defense of his life as "part of society-at-large" and especially his charge that in Toby's world there was "nothing to mock at, no jokes" (par. 23). (If we've read "Protestant" I refer back to Keillor's Brethren, his gently joking tone and the potential aura of blasphemy that hovers over it.) Are there beliefs and practices so serious, so holy that there is no room for jokes? I find this useful to lead into a discussion of what may seem to be the almost universal "lightness" of our society, where, for many, perhaps most, nothing is serious, nothing outside the realm of jokes, nothing that Saturday Night Live or Monty Python can't take on. It's interesting to see what advantages and disadvantages students claim for or charge against the casual and the laid-back.

I then try to get the class to see how Bleilip romanticizes the community, the survivors, and seems to have come to it for answers, miracles, while at the same time rejecting it. (I have them read through pars. 27 and 31 carefully, sentence by sentence.)

I have to take my classes very carefully too through the long paragraphs 36 and 37 and the conversation that follows (pausing, sometimes, at the end of 36 with the "dirty tablecloth--no vestments, altars, sacrifices" to compare it to the Brethren in "Protestant," and, perhaps,

to compare the preceding ritual to Keillor's attraction
to the Roman Catholic services). Try to get them to point
out that it is not the description of the ancient ritual
but the desperate interpretation of it and of the world
as slaughterhouse that the rebbe says he took from
Bleilip's "liver." Despite their fundamentalism, the
Hasidim--and the experiences of the survivors in the
deathcamps--believe the world is not in vain but a realm
of joy.
    The most difficult concept for my students is that
which insists the toy gun is more dangerous than the
loaded real one. I have some trouble with that myself,
but I try to apply the rebbe's second-hand story from
par. 76; that the toy is pretense, ashes, nonreality or
death, and the loaded gun, though lethal, is real and
therefore of the world. (How do you read that? I'm not
too sure I got it all.)
    But I'm not sure the last paragraph, in which the
rebbe says that Bleilip's periods of belief make him as
bloody as anyone, is not equally difficult. The rebbe and
his father had moments of disbelief, so the rebbe is not
sure of the temple ritual (which is not to say for sure
that he does not think it proper), but since Bleilip does
have moments of belief, he is as guilty of the blood of
sacrifice as anyone--that is, if he needs God, he needs
Scripture and ritual--and therefore may need sacrifice.
    Working through the difficulties--the story is
powerful enough to be worth it--we can then come to the
ultimate question, the question Bleilip asks himself,
"Was it amazing chance that the rebbe had challenged the
contents of his pockets, or was he a seer?" What is the
register of reality--and superreality--in this story?
(See the discussion of "Summer Water and Shirley.")


                    Barry Targan
                     DOMINION

Short story; Jewish-American
    So will it be Cornell or Yale?
    Those of us who are parents or are of parental age
will probably not have much difficulty empathizing with
the father in this story, and the centered consciousness
of the father brings most of the students along. But not
all. Some--and not just those who have gone through some
sort of conversion experience which has separated them in
some way or another from their family--think Poverman
unduly interferes in his son's life, that the story is
regressive. I confess I was taken aback at first, the
case here seems so clear. But I've been taught by my
students to change the terms a little--suppose the family
were devotees of some weird cult, or neo-Nazis: does the
son, even a son of high school age, have the right to

choose his own life, his own beliefs? I agree that's a different story, as it were, an abstraction or generalization of generational questions from a story that is particular, but you might want to be prepared. (I don't bring this up, but I have both barrels loaded just in case.)

I begin with something else, suggested in the first part of the third study question: what does the first part of the story, that portion concerning Charney and the bankruptcy, have to do with the second half, which concerns Robert? It seems clear that Robert is not thinking of not attending university because of the financial burden on his family, though that is what some of my students want to say at first. What has happened to Poverman in the first part of the story? I ask. It doesn't take long to make clear the fact that he has lost his money, that Charney is responsible, but that Poverman is relatively calm and almost frustratingly forgiving and passive. In the second part of the story he thinks he is in danger of losing his son, and is far from passive. So I play on this: what does that mean about what he thinks of money? of his son? and so on.

I pretty much let my students have their heads when it comes to discussing the Society of the Holy Word. Generally they have had more experience with such groups--being recruited or involved--than I have and know what to look for and how to read this portion of the story. There are some who, again, find Poverman, like Keillor and others, blasphemous, but I can usually rely on the rest of the class--certainly by this time--to judge the Society fairly accurately, or at least to see what Poverman finds and fears.

When this has been thrashed out, I turn to par. 195 and what follows. I have them read the paragraph sentence by sentence, covering as much as I can of the "business" imagery, the colloquial language ("scram") next to the more formal or Biblical ("vaunt"), and inferring the determination Poverman has made. I dip down into the parenthesis in par. 202 "(cotton/polyester--60/40, not silk)" and ask why that is there--it doesn't take long for its relation to Poverman's business and its implication of inelegance, impurity, maybe even tackiness to transfer from the robe to the Society.

Parent that I am, I find it moving that Robert breaks in when his father is abasing himself, calling himself "a bad man stained with sin." Most of my students, however, are, I am glad to say, with me, and say that they would probably react as Robert does. (To impersonalize it a bit, I suggest that what we learn about Poverman from the inside and from his actions makes us reluctant to have him confess to being "bad.")

I ask about the imagery in the final paragraph to try to get them to suggest that it is religious. I hope they argue that the father's attack is not upon religion or God, but upon what he thinks of as a false or feeble religious cult, destructive of his son's earthly life without saving his immortal soul. Fighting for his son, indeed, is not without glory, no matter how uneasily we might at first have thought the word sat on poor Poverman's head.

Estela Portillo
THE DAY OF THE SWALLOWS

Play; Chicana
<u>Stage</u> <u>Directions</u> <u>and</u> <u>Scene</u> 1

I find it worthwhile the day before assigning <u>The Day of the Swallows</u> to spend fifteen minutes or so having the introductory paragraphs read aloud, one by one, in class, asking mostly about tone and expectations. How does the first paragraph end? I ask. The second? "Here it [the lake] drinks the sun in madness" and "No one dares ask for life" don't seem to promise comedy or romance (despite the romantic setting). And all that about werewolf hearts and biting into passion sets up even the casual reader. If I have time left, I go on with the two paragraphs setting up scene 1. The contrast of the first scene with what precedes it should raise some questions. (My more perceptive students seem to expect this beautiful room to somehow be threatened by the barrio-- the conquered conquering the conquerors. Which only goes to prove that perceptive readers get more out of a text but do not necessarily guess the outcome correctly.) Most of my students, trained by television and movies "know" that what Alysea is doing is washing blood out of the carpet. This is a good place to leave them; they're almost sure now to read on.

I suggest, however, that when they finish the first scene they pause and think back and project forward before going on. I often have them keep a reading journal with each entry dated and timed. A fair number, I find, catch on to such red herrings as Alysea looking at her hands when Clemencia is there; it is perfectly natural in the light of what she is doing, but it does cast suspicion on her as the spiller of blood (and my students feel that where there's blood, there's a murder). At the end of the scene I ask them whether they believe Alysea or Josefa about David's fate and future. I also ask them about the last line of the scene, "Anything . . . anything is worth this!" What's "this"? What do they think "anything" portends?

My students are suspicious of Josefa right away. She's too good to be true and they are leary of people who talk about patterning "our lives for one beautiful moment," though they are quick to pick up the simile-- "like this lace . . . little bits and pieces come together . . . "--and write SYMBOL in the margin. So I have to defend Josefa and stress her beauty and sensitivity; after all, the play would lack passion if we didn't care what happened to her.

By the time they have read the first scene students should have noticed the symbolic insistence on lace and light and will probably have some idea of what they mean to Josefa and the play.

Act I, Scene 2

I don't usually like to carry on the stop-and-go reading technique I use to talk about expectations. However, the scene with Eduardo raises many possibilities, especially that he and Josefa might have a relationship. He also introduces elements other than plot that raise expectations, such as calling the room a room for women, suggesting that Josefa will not like his taking Alysea away as his "squaw," and setting up a binary opposition between the room and "the open." I ask students what associations they have with inside and outside here, and, since this chapter, after all, deals with myth, symbol, and religion, call attention to Father Prado's approval of the "holier temple" among the pines. I also ask them to focus on the conversation between Josefa and Eduardo when they are alone and gloss the implied meanings of sea and lake, whirlwind, barrio, desert, and especially when Alysea returns, the magicians. Sometimes I ask a couple of students to read the parts.

I get mixed responses to Josefa's description of her mystical experience. Those who find her language pretentious find this somewhat silly; those who accept her as sensitive and mysterious find this passage moving. It is an especially good passage to have performed, preferably repeatedly performed, by different students to wring all the possible tones and meanings out of it.

If I give two class periods to the play--and I usually do--the first assignment ends with the second scene. It is therefore another good place to test expectations, especially since Tomas has returned with David's horse. Moreover, the fact that Josefa crippled the man who was chasing Alysea and left David's drunken father to die darkens the picture of her and makes the mystery of what happened to David even more ominous. And Tomas? What role will he play later on?

Act I, Scene 3

Clara, the aging beauty put aside by her lover for a younger woman and turning to drink, is something of a stock figure, though it takes me a while to get that out of a class. I then try to turn the tables a bit and challenge them "as actresses" to breathe new life or depth or individuality into the part by their reading. What comes out, when it comes, usually has to do with her relationship to her rival, Alysea, though once I got a new angle from a student who had Clara read "My downfall? [In a whisper.] My life?" in such a way as to suggest a certain amount of fear of, along with admiration for, Josefa.

This is also a good scene with which to play the expectation game. I usually end the first assignment with scene 2, but you might prefer the division Portillo herself made and divide the assignment by acts so that this would be the point at which to pause, take stock, and project. (A theatre audience would have to pause here for intermission rather than after scene 2. Come to think of it, maybe I should make the division here next time.)

Act II
In the previous scene and in the early lines of this act more and more is being said about the magicians. I sometimes have students as they go through the play collect references to the magicians sequentially and try to frame descriptions or definitions after each set or group of appearances of the term. I suggest that this framing of a definition, a configuration, is wholly analogous to framing expectation, making some kind of shape or whole out of the fragments we gather as we read. The projected definitions of the magicians get particularly interesting when Don Esquinas reports that Clara said Josefa's magicians have no faces. I have had some success as well asking students to keep similar configurations of Josefa's character, that is, periodically stopping and trying to define just what kind of a person she is. That exercise too gets particularly intriguing in the early stages of the final act; when Tomas suggests he knows about Josefa and Alysea, for example, or when Don Esquinas says Josefa has done enough harm to Clara already, supplying her with liquor and "lies" (and all this after the tender scene with the injured bird).

A few of my students have had some difficulty relating "putting ugliness away" and "atonement," so you might want to get that connection on the table early in discussing the scene.

The scene with Don Esquinas, besides his accusations about Josefa's harming Clara, may be a good point at which to review the gender issue, starting with Josefa's frequent attacks on men and their ways. If you have assigned the first act as the first day's assignment, before your students read the final act you may want to have this scene read aloud in class. Review the treatment of gender in the play at this point before the denouement, and even before Tomas's revelations later in the scene.

What do your students make of Josefa's final speech in act II? What is the new birth of light? Who or what is Josefa's lover? The moon? magicians? (It is not until well into act II that we learn she means the lake.)

## Act III

I sometimes use the exchange between Josefa and Father Prado on the festival to reopen the discussion on ritual (which I have usually generated earlier). In the exchange, he asks if it isn't true that the festival for her is "just ritual," and she responds that for the barrio people it is rebirth. Father Prado clearly means ritual, repeated ceremony divorced from its religious meaning. Josefa gives it new religious meaning, rebirth into life and joy and belief, perhaps. I ask the class to recall the polishing of the abalone, the burial of urns, the dance with the eagle-feather fan, the sacrifice of the goat and bullock, even the anti-ritual of the Brethren in a kind of review of the chapter.

If you dare, before your students have read this final act, you might have them read the beginning of Josefa's confession. Go through the longish speech that begins "Last night . . . last night . . . ," or even down to Josefa's "I told her . . . go with me when the moon comes out . . . ," and have them recount what they think Josefa did to David. Do you think this red herring, as it were, is intended; that we are supposed to think that Josefa, a man-hater we know by now, castrated him? If so, how do you read the real event . . . ?

You might want to ask your students how they understand Father Prado's feelings of guilt at not understanding that underneath Josefa's calm exterior there were "twisted fears." How do they understand the final thirty lines or so in which Father Prado sees much God in her and she says instead she is the "high priestess" of the light her magicians gave her? I'm not sure I could paraphrase all this and certainly not all its implications, but it can make for a good class period, a cooperative exploration.

## Final Scene

Father Prado reportedly said Josefa is like a cathedral, like the silence of the cathedral, the stained-glass windows her soul. She says her magicians will let her come back as light and the final stage direction dictates choir voices, church bells, birds in full life, and light that is almost unearthly. All this seems to celebrate Josefa's suicide and virtually authorize or underwrite her vision, her belief in "magicians," and so on. How does your class respond to that? (How do you?) I don't know whether you want to get into this, but so many independent or unconventional women in fiction (including drama) end up committing suicide--Emma Bovary by poison, Anna Karenina under the train--and not only those created by male authors. Kate Chopin's Edna Pontellier, like Portillo's here, drowns herself (a gentler and symbolically more "feminine" ending, perhaps). Is this the measure of the hopelessness of female freedom in a patriarchal society? or, analogously, the only ending imaginable for the writer writing in such a society (since it is difficult for him or her to imagine a wholly happy ending for such a "misfit")?